SILENCE AT THE CENTER OF TIME

ESSAYS

J.D. GILL, PH.D.

CREATE SPACE
2018

"I dined with Legrandin on the terrace of his house by moonlight. "There is a charming quality, is there not," he said to me, "in this silence; for hearts that are wounded, as mine is, a novelist whom you will read in time to come asserts that there is no remedy but silence and shadow. And you see this, my boy, there comes in all our lives a time, towards which you still have far to go, when the weary eyes can endure but one kind of light, the light which a fine evening like this prepares for us in the stillroom for darkness, when the ears can listen to no music save what the moonlight breathes through the flute of silence."

—Marcel Proust *Swan's Way*

CONTENTS

THE EMPTY SELF

The person I want to describe is essentially born into a context that has no place for him or her. That is, the mother is largely focused on herself. The child exists not in his or her own right as a person, but as an extension of the thoughts and wishes of the mother. The child is "mother's little angel," "the next genius," &c.

The child fulfills a *role* in the mind of the mother. He or she is not considered as a real person by her. The mother sees the child in terms of the role that child plays in the mother's economy.

Such a mother does not seek to establish a resonant bond with the child's separate thoughts and emotions. Nor does she value these things. She values her own thoughts and emotions.

If the parent-child interaction is not primarily based on resonance and a welcoming inclusion of who each other is, the focus of that interaction will fall to behavior. The major concern in this situation will be how the child behaves. In this there will likely be a right way and a wrong way.

When the primary focus is on how the child behaves instead of on who he or she is, the child's self is largely ignored, and the child is treated as an object.

The old dictum that the child is to be seen and not heard is an instance of this kind of objectification. Other versions are the amount of energy expended to make sure the child is seen to be a certain proper sort of way by others—instead of allowing the child to express his or her own wants and desires.

This distinction is important, because, right at the start, the child either learns he or she matters or else it is the child's actions and appearance that matters.

A child who is allowed to be who he or she is will be able to be that person in multiple contexts. On the other hand, a child who has been taught to do the right thing will tend to behave in ways the context approves.

The difference here is between a child who "gets to be who *he or she* is" versus a child who "has to do what *they* want."

If the child's self, as he or she knows it, is not accepted by the parent, the child will need to create a self that can be accepted. This is how narcissistic structure begins.

Of course, there are limits to acceptable behavior in different contexts. I am not arguing for the training of a child who runs amok. The difference I am trying to illuminate is one between a family that welcomes each member as who they are into the functioning unit versus a family that holds all members to a code of conduct.

The welcoming family tends to be more *open*. The code of conduct family tends to be more *closed*. Exploring new possibilities will occur more often in the open family, whereas conforming to the *right* code will occur more often in the closed family.

An infant that is born into a family in which the infant feels 1) safe and 2) welcome will tend to develop a secure attachment pattern (Bowlby, 1988, Fonagy, 2001). *It is important how the infant exists in the mother's mind.* If the mother is delighted in the child for who the child is, the child will tend to develop a positive sense of self-worth. This follows from the fact the child is being treated as one of worth.

We may say such an infant is *found* by his or her mother and treated like the person found.

Such a child will tend to see the world as a welcoming place and to feel that he or she has a place in it. This has consequences for the child's interpersonal experiences as well as later school and work performance.

If the child is not found by the mother and does not experience an interpersonal emotional resonance with the mother, the mother herself tends to function as an object in the world of the child. Everything tends to be an object. And, the child learns, objects interact with each other in patterned ways. Objects also have relative value to each other.

That is if the child is not found by the mother, he or she will not be able to find a reflection of him or herself as a *person* in the mind of the mother. Such a child will find him or herself to be a certain kind of object (a "good kid," "a royal pain," &c.).

The child will learn that appearing to be a wonderful object is better than appearing to be an ordinary object. Behind either of these, however, the child's real self remains devalued and under-developed.

Since there is not a development of an interior sense of self in such a child, the only option for identity is an exterior sense of self. That is the child is not so much who he or she knows him or herself to be, but the child is who others know him or her to be.

In such a case if one succeeds then one is a worthwhile child. If one does not succeed, then one is not worthwhile. One's status depends on how one's behavior is viewed by others. This is the situation Rogers (1995) called "conditions of worth." That is, one's worth depends on what one does, not who one is.

Gibson (2015) wrote:

> At heart, children of narcissists, raised up or
> cast down by the ever-evaluating parent, feel
> themselves to be less than nothing because

they must "be" something to earn their parents' love. Conditional love offers no support for the inner self. It creates people who have no personal sense of substance or worth. Nourished on conditional love, children of narcissists become conditional. They find themselves unreal (pp. 14, 15).

If society worships such external things as how you appear to others, your status, power, and money, a person may acquire the belief that what she keeps inside, her emotions and the deeds that only she knows about, do not count. Yet the only real and lasting sense of self-worth that a person can have is the feeling of and for her essential self, the sense of being real, of doing what possibly she alone thinks appropriate. Having an appreciation of the subjective intangible is what we mean when we say that someone has "character," a rare trait today (Ibid. p. 19).

Applying the values of an externalized society to one's self causes narcissistic wounding...When love depends on externals, on others' opinions of what you are and do, the self is betrayed (Ibid).

Each narcissistic parent in each generation repeats the crime that was perpetrated against him or her. The crime is non-acceptance (Ibid. p. 20).

Such a child, instead of developing a secure sense of self that feels welcome in the world, will develop a self that is contingent on how it performs and how it is seen by others.

There will be an emptiness at the core of such a child.

What will surround the child are judgments about behavior. The child will live in a world of right and wrong behaviors. These dimensions, as seen in the child's family, will be internalized by the child. It will be these judgements that the child will carry forth into his or her life instead of the welcoming acceptance of being found.

When right and wrong judgements comprise the majority of the child's context, avoiding wrong or negative judgements will become an important pursuit.

Of course, there are children who seek negative judgements in order to frustrate parents and others who have hurt them. Such children sacrifice themselves on the altar of denying parents the opportunity to think they are good parents.

If my focus is on avoiding as many negative judgements as possible, it will likely occur to me that one way this could happen would be if I were *perfect*. Being perfect means, no negative judgements are possible. I may internalize a quest for perfection, though this may not be clearly recognized.

The problem with this is that I am human and therefore incapable of being perfect. The internalized judgement that I lack perfection will be a constant source of torment to me, as it is a criterion I can never achieve.

The result is an empty self with a severe internal judge.

Golomb (1995) wrote:

> For many years, wherever I went, I was accompanied by a gang of harsh critics who made my life almost unbearable. No matter what I tried to accomplish, they were always there reminding me that I wasn't up to the task and could never do a good enough job (p. 3).

> ...[these harsh critics] created such an extreme sensitivity in me that I constantly assumed others were judging me as critically as I was judging myself (Ibid. p. 4).

> [What was missing]...was the nurturing and empathetic love that we all desperately needed—but didn't get—from our mothers. And our mothers probably hadn't gotten it from their mother, either, which means that a painful legacy of distorted love was passed from generation to generation (Ibid. p. 6).

In this situation there is a right way to do things. This right way will have been determined by the person's context. Thoughts of changing contexts will be highly worrisome as one won't know the rules of the new context and will thus be at a disadvantage.

If one finds oneself in a new context, the experience is likely to lead one to feeling lonely and anxious. This is true, because one won't have a developed self upon which to rely—and one won't know the new rules well.

Such a child will tend to be a closed adult. He or she will treat his or her own child in the known way. This will be as an object that needs to behave properly.

The empty self and the closed adult will tend to be surrounded by fear. "What if I make a mistake?" "What if I am wrong about something?" "What if someone finds out I feel like a worthless nobody inside?" Such thoughts will tend to be paralyzing.

If the closed adult finds a place in a system where the rules are dictated and can be followed, he or she will likely be able to function in an acceptable fashion. This pattern will be able to continue until a situation arises for which there is not a correct answer or a known way to behave.

In fact, such a situation will recur with some frequency simply due to the fact that reality is dynamic instead of static and change is always afoot.

Gibson (2015) wrote:

If [parents] don't make a solid emotional connection with their child, the child will have a gaping hole where security might have been...The loneliness of feeling unseen by others is as fundamental a pain as physical injury, but it doesn't show on the outside (p. 7).

Children have no way of identifying a lack of emotional intimacy in their relationship with a parent (Ibid).

[Also]...if your parent was scared [afraid] of deep feelings, you might have been left with an uneasy sense of shame for needing comforting (Ibid. p. 8).

A lack of emotional intimacy creates emotional loneliness in children and adults. Attentive and reliable emotional relationships are the basis of a child's sense of security...Parental neglect and rejection in childhood can adversely affect self-confidence and relationships in adulthood, as people repeat old, frustrating patterns and then blame themselves for not being happy (Ibid. p. 24).

The above pattern is different when the empty self is predatory.

In this case the child has not only been treated as an object but also has been subjected to sadism. That is, the parent enjoyed hurting the deviant child.

In this case the child will have the feeling of having been *done to*. That is, the child will develop a resentment. This changes the child from feeling *separate* to feeling *against*. The goal will now be to get something from the other.

This is the outcome Kimmel (2013) called *aggrieved entitlement*. One feels one is owed for the abuse one has suffered.

It is in this context one may seek a partner who can be treated abusively in order to work out one's anger.

It is not uncommon for a person in the presence of an overtly narcissistic individual to routinely feel *inadequate* or *less* than the narcissistic individual. That is, the other will seem greater, in charge, difficult to please, touchy, and demanding.

On the other hand, a person in the presence of a covertly narcissistic individual will routinely feel *burdened*. The other person needs so much, and if these supplies are not given, the other will feel denied, bereft, and abandoned.

The anger is worked out either way. It is always the other who is not giving, not the narcissistic person. And through the mechanism of projective identification, the other will feel inadequate as well.

Of course, there are individual variations of these patterns, and they rarely present in pure form.

One severe variation is the result of what Green (see Kohon, 1999) called The Dead Mother. This is a mother who is physically present but psychologically absent—or "dead."

Modell (1999) wrote:

> In some instances, it would appear as if their mother was unable to recognize that her child had an inner life that was separate and distinct from her own. [...] The consequences of experiencing this failure [...] can be devastating. For recognizing the uniqueness of children's inner life is equivalent to recognizing that they are psychically alive. It is as if their mothers failed to acknowledge their humanity [...] The child has not been granted the permission to be a person [which] may result in the conviction that all desires are forbidden, for if one does have a right to exist one has no right to have desires, to want anything for oneself. (p.77-78)

Left without a working sense of self, the child identifies with the mother—who exists as a kind of non-person herself.

It was Bowlby (2005) who suggested that the primitive part of the psyche feels that safety lies in familiarity.

Modell (Ibid) adds:

> This total identification with a dead mother who is incapable of loving contributes to a corresponding incapacity to love others and love oneself. (p.78)

Such a child has not had an experience of being with another person—only with an object. Relationship is known only in object-like terms. In this situation the person will show to the loved one the empty non-connection he or she experienced as a child. The emptiness is thus passed along.

Freud (1964) gave a classic description of the process of identification with a lost person.

> There is no difficulty in reconstructing this process. An object-choice, an attachment of the libido to a particular person, had at one time existed; then, owing to a real slight or disappointment coming from this loved person, the object-relationship was shattered. The result was not the normal one of a withdrawal of the libido from this object and a displacement of it on to a new one, but something different, for whose

coming-about various conditions seem to be necessary. [Here] the free libido was not displaced on to another object; it was withdrawn into the ego. There, however, it was not employed in any unspecified way, but served to establish an *identification* of the ego with the abandoned object. Thus, the shadow of the object fell upon the ego, and the latter could henceforth be judged by a special agency, as though it were an object, the forsaken object. In this way an object-loss was transformed into an ego-loss and the conflict between the ego and the loved person into a cleavage between the critical activity of the ego and the ego as altered by identification (p. 248-249).

The result of this process is that the person criticizes and is hostile to him or herself, effectively punishing the self for the loss. That is, the rejecting other becomes a part of the self. This part then attacks the self and rejects it.

Treatment is difficult as patients tend to not improve beyond a certain basic point. Being treated empathically by a therapist is experienced as a nice, but not curative interaction. Such patients can never decide what they want to do. This is not because they can't think of something to do, but more because *they don't know where they are starting from*. That is, they don't know how to be the author of something; they only know how to fit in.

Coming to an awareness of one's situation is very difficult for these types of patients. The demand for perfection is routinely not conscious. An idea of what a workable sense of self might be seems beyond imagination. Further, empty self patients routinely are surrounded by other empty self people, and thus everything seems ordinary—if miserable.

Explaining in an open and compassionate way how the empty self develops may provide for an opening. The child has been treated as an object instead of a person who has thoughts and feelings. That is the parent related to the child's exteriority instead of the child's interiority. Consequently, the interiority did not develop.

Therapy is an experience that can be curative. This is true for several reasons. First, the therapist is a different person than the parents. The therapist, therefore, can offer a different context than the parents could. Secondly, the therapist is an expert in empathy (feeling with). The therapist can contact and resonate with the patient in a way the parent could not do.

Third, the therapist does not need the patient to be a reflection of the therapist. Thus, the patient can be respected for being precisely who he or she is. Fourth, the therapist is not a judge. Fifth, the therapist can help the patient discover who he or she is in the context of the therapeutic encounter.

For these reasons, the patient finds him or herself in a context that is different from his or her childhood context and is treated in a nonjudgmental fashion as a person of worth regardless of who he or she happens to be.

The patient may feel empty inside but present an all-capable, adequate, and manipulative facade. There is considerable effort expended to keep the inner experience hidden. Or the patient may simply feel empty and ineffectual. Here, there exists the same degree of entitlement and tendency to exploitation, but there is also a history of ineffective functioning, failed hopes, and interpersonal stress.

While overt narcissists are easy to spot with their grandiosity and displays of superiority (to conceal an inner sense of vulnerability), covert narcissists are less theatrical. These people, especially initially, tend to be observers. They, however, observe from a sense of superiority as well as aloof detachment and general inattentiveness.

In reality both these kinds of people are highly critical and dismissive. They tend to avoid close, open interactions as they routinely hold others in contempt. They are the petunia in the onion patch.

The difference between covert narcissists and introverts is that introverts are typically good listeners. Covert narcissists, on the other hand, are not interested in anything that differs from their own views and needs.

Narcissistic persons can operate in a passive-aggressive pattern in order to seem agreeable, but at the same time only operate on their own interests. Many narcissists are exquisitely sensitive to any slight, withdrawing from the negative situation to protect their developed aloofness.

Withdrawal into a kind of "splendid isolation" protects the vulnerable self at the same time prevents others from discovering the narcissistic person's interpersonal inadequacies.

What is missing is the ability to be found. The real status of the self must be disguised at all costs.

In ordinary development, one starts out as a beginner and then progresses as far as one can. Narcissistic people, on the other hand, conceal the beginner's uncertainty and simply adopt a polished facade from the start. They have not had the experience of being found and admired for who they are—beginner to expert. As detailed above the inner inadequacy is a source of shame and personal disavowal.

Some people are simply predatory. Behind their mask of a shy, "good person," a far more sinister truth resides. There is a presentation of a person they inwardly feel they are not. Such persons may show a different "face" to each person they meet. It is also likely those closest to them see a different person than strangers see. The person may be a monster at home and sweet and friendly outside of the home.

When problems arise in a relationship, it is routinely the other who is held to blame. The narcissistic person typically feels he or she had done nothing to deserve reproach. Such people can be astonishing liars. The reason for this is that lying and misrepresentation are tools of survival and, hence, are not hooked to the shame system.

Faced with clear evidence of their lies, these people are able to use a complex of defense mechanisms including denial, reframing, sliding word meanings, as well as attempting to blame the other for the problem.

It is routinely the case narcissistic persons have a feeling of being betrayed by the world that stubbornly refuses to recognize their superiority and inherent capacity. Such persons routinely display vulnerability as well as hypersensitivity. They have unfulfilled expectations and are vulnerable to stress. Sometimes there is a lack of zest for work (narcissistic deficiency). Feelings of shame are common.

Shyness and introversion are different from covert narcissism. Shy people are typically anxious and neurotic. Introverts, on the other hand, routinely enjoy alone time and are not anxious around others.

In short, the two types of narcissism, overt and covert, share the common features of grandiosity and arrogance as well as self focus and lack of working empathy. It may be said that in extreme cases overt narcissists are predators whereas covert narcissists are prey.

There is a significant relationship between covert narcissism and co-dependency. This is the case as abusive, narcissistic parenting is a factor in producing co-dependent children.

McBride (2009) wrote:

> When mothers are narcissistic, they control their child's interests and activities so that they revolve around what the mothers find interesting, convenient, or nonthreatening. They do not encourage what their daughters truly want or need (p. 23).

In this process the mother trains the child to provide supplies to the mother and to sublimate their own identities to those of the mother. This prevents the child from developing a functional personality of his or her own.

Co-dependent people are drawn to narcissists for the drama they provide. Other people are simply seen as boring. In fact, covert narcissistic people may respond like overt narcissists when they are with a non-narcissistic partner.

Narcissistic people routinely do not accept responsibility for their behavior. They blame others, fate, &c. Further such narcissistic people can never be sated. They always need more.

An excess emphasis on appearance is often found. This draws attention and approval. Having the "right" stuff (clothes, house, &c.) does the same. Sexuality is used as a tool to secure supplies, not as an act in itself. That is, true nakedness (i.e., open intimacy) is avoided in the service of protecting the false self.

Such people are a disaster as a parent. The child is not seen and loved for who he or she is. On the contrary, the child is seen as an extension of the parent. That is, how the child behaves is a direct reflection on the parent. Again, the parents need the child to be an element in his or her psychic economy instead of an independent human being.

This has at least two effects: 1) the child is robbed of developing a coherent sense of self. 2) the child will have false-self functioning modeled in the home as ordinary behavior. Such a child will grow up to have an empty sense of self that must be covered up by some sort of manipulative behavior.

McBride (2009) argued:

> A daughter who doesn't receive validation from her earliest relationship with her mother learns that she has no significance in the world and her efforts have no effect. She…thinks…the problem…lies within herself (Ibid, p. 7).

There are further issues that develop as the child grows into adulthood.

The first of these has to do with the effects of long term trauma on the brain. Repeated trauma leads to anxiety, post-traumatic stress disorder, and complex post-traumatic stress disorder. Specifically, ongoing exposure to stress shrinks the hippocampus (which plays a part in memory and learning). At the same time the amygdala is enlarged (which plays a part in fear, guilt, grief, and shame).

Goleman (2006) argued:

> The hippocampus, near the amygdala in the mid-brain, is our central organ for learning. This structure enables us to convert the content of 'working memory'—new information held briefly in the prefrontal cortex—into long-term form for storage. This neural act is the heart of learning. Once our mind connects this information with what we already know, we will be able to bring the new understanding to mind weeks or years later. (p. 273)

Stress tends to short-circuit the higher cognitive functions.

> When we are under stress, the HPA axis roars into action, preparing the body for crisis. Among other biological maneuvers, the amygdala commandeers the prefrontal cortex, the brain's executive center. This shift in control to the low road favors automatic habits, as the amygdala draws on our knee-jerk responses to save us. The

thinking brain gets sidelined for the
duration; the high road moves too slowly.
(Ibid, p. 268)

Persons with high baseline cortisol, a major stress
hormone, have been shown to have lower hippocampal
volume over time (see H).

Being in an ongoing relationship with a narcissistic
person involves experiencing high levels of anxiety and
fear. This is true as narcissistic persons routinely punish
those who do not live up to their expectations and demands.

This implies that persons who are involved with
narcissistic individuals experience flight or fight symptoms
almost daily. In addition to immediate events, subliminal
and unconscious hints related to prior wounds are able to
trigger the flight or fight sequence and the release of
cortisol.

Goleman (2017) stated:

The hippocampus is especially vulnerable to
ongoing emotional distress, because of the
damaging effects of cortisol (Ibid, p. 273).

This can have profound effects on learning as
cortisol affects the rate at which neurons are either
added or subtracted from the hippocampus. In this

situation *duration* of stress is almost equal to *extent* of stress.

> Cortisol stimulates the amygdala while it impairs the hippocampus, forcing our attention onto the emotions we feel, while restricting our ability to take in new information" (Ibid, pp. 273-274).

> The neural highway for dysphoria [4] runs from the amygdala to the right side of the prefrontal cortex. As this circuitry activates, our thoughts fixate on what has triggered the distress. And as we become preoccupied, say, with worry or resentment, our mental agility sputters. Likewise, when we are sad, activity levels in the prefrontal cortex drop and we generate fewer thoughts. Extremes of anxiety and anger on the one hand and sadness on the other push brain activity beyond its zones of effective-ness (Ibid, p. 268).

The abuse experienced in such situations can be extreme.

> Studies in rats and primates suggest that glucocorticoids, the equivalent of cortisol in other species, "may be neurotoxic to the

hippocampus at the massive levels that are released under extreme stress or during trauma," said Dr. Robert Sapolsky, a neuroscientist at Stanford University. "I'm talking about the levels you would see in a zebra running from a lion, or a person fleeing a mugger -- a real physical life-and-death crisis -- if it is repeated again and again as time goes on (see Goleman, Ibid)."

The second effect that may be found as the child matures into adulthood is that childhood abuse can become adult self-abuse.

In this situation how the child sees him or herself is dependent on the actions, attitudes, and viewpoints of the people around the child.

When the child suffers a significant trauma, it may go unnoticed by those surrounding the child. In this situation the child is unable to process the trauma properly as he or she lacks adult capacities. The child may dissociate the trauma or he or she may internalize the trauma as a *normal* part of life.

This is compounded when it is the parent who is the cause of the child's trauma. The adult, not wanting to accept responsibility for this trauma, may blame the child. "You are bad." In other cases, the child may be rejected or ignored (the silent treatment).

In our culture parents are privileged over the child. "These are your parents after all." "They didn't mean to." "It was the times." "You must respect your parents," &c.

The child may think "Why don't you love me?" "Why do you ignore my thoughts and feelings?"

In time these thoughts morph into self punitive and self-debasing thoughts such as: "I am unlovable," "I am worthless, &c."

In extreme situations such thoughts can lead to self-harm and even suicide.

This is to say the rage, hurt, sadness, and fear—having been experienced and not worked through—remain as internalized truths upon which the child will construct an identity. "This is who I am."

If the child is unable to work through these thoughts and feelings with another person, in another kind of context, they are simply accepted as reality.

REFERENCES

Ashbach, C. A Reversible Perspective: Who the Subject?...Who the Object. IPI Presentation, 03-11-17.

Bowlby, J. A Secure Base. Hogarth, 2005.

Bowlby, J. A Secure Base: Parent-Child Attachment and Healthy Human Development. Basic, 1988.

Bremner, J.D. Stressing the Hippocampus: Why it Matters. Scientific American. https://blogs.scientificamerican.com/news-blog/stressing-the-hippocampus-why-it-ma/

Cooper, J., and Maxwell, N. Narcissistic Wounds. Aronson, 1995.

Fonagy, P. Attachment Theory and Psychoanalysis. Other, 2001.

Forney, M. Why You Should Beware of "Inverted" Narcisstic Women. http://www.returnofkings.com/90052/why-you-should-beware-of-inverted-narcissist-women

Forward, S., and Buck, C. Toxic Parents: Overcoming Their Hurtful Legacy and Reclaiming Your Life. Bantam, 2002.

Freud, S. Mourning and Melancholia in The Standard Edition of the Complete Psychological Works of Sigmund Freud. Trans J. Strachey. Vol XIV, Hogarth, 1964.

Gabbard, G.O. Psychodynamic Psychology in Clinical Practice. APA, 1994.

Gibson, L. Adult Children of Emotionally Immature Parents. New Harbinger, 2015.

Goleman, D. Severe Trauma may Damage the Brain as well as the Psyche. New York Times, 8-1-17.

Golomb, E. Trapped in the Mirror: Adult Children of Narcissists in their Struggle for Self. Morrow, 1995.

Goodhardt, C. D. A Primer for ICD-10-CM Users. APA, 2014.

Gross, G. Effects of Stress on the Hippocampus. http://drgailgross.com/academia/effects-of-stress-on-the-hippocampus/

Kimmel, M. Angry White Men: American Masculinity at the End of an Era. Nation, 2013.

Kohon, G. (Ed.) The Dead Mother: The Work of Andre Green. New Library of Psychoanalysis, 1999.

Kohut, H. How Does Psychoanalysis Cure? Chicago, 1984.

Lingiardi, V., and McWilliams, N. (Eds.) Psychodynamic Diagnostic Manual, Second Edition: PDM-2. Guilford, 2017.

McBride, K. Will I Ever Be Good Enough: Healing the Daughters of Narcissistic Mothers. Atria Books; Reprint edition, 2009.

McWilliams, N. Psychoanalytic Diagnosis: Understanding Personality Structures in the Clinical Process. Guilford, 1994.

Mitchell, S. A. Influence and Autonomy in Psychoanalysis. Routledge, 1997.

Modell, A. H. The Dead Mother Syndrome and the Reconstruction of Trauma. In the Dead Mother: The Work of Andre Green. G. Kohon (Ed.), New Library of Psychoanalysis, 1999.

Mollen, P. The Fragile Self. Aronson, 1993.

Rogers, C., and Kramer, P.D. On Becoming a Person: A Therapist's View of Psychotherapy. Mariner, 1995.

Symington, N., and Symington, J. The Clinical Thinking of Wilfred Bion. Routledge, 1996.

Thomas, E. The Amygdala & Emotions. http://www.effective-mind-control.com/amygdala.html

Vaknin, S. Malignant Self-Love: Narcissism Revisited. Narcissus Publications. Tenth Edition, 2015.

FENCES

"Something there is that doesn't love a wall," wrote Robert Frost in a famous poem. The speaker of the poem was nevertheless there, mending the wall with his more orderly neighbor. The neighbor holds: "Good fences make good neighbors." Frost, as speaker, thinks

> Before I built a wall I'd ask to know
> What I was walling in or walling out

The poem, "Mending Wall," suggests a contrast between older tradition and newer thinking (Frost, 1914/1973). The neighbor is content to follow the old ways. Frost, as speaker in the poem, is not so sure.

What of this difference between those who are sure and those who are not so sure? Is there a virtue to be found in uncertainty?

Further, what if certainty and uncertainty were essentially linked to fear? Would higher fear result in a greater need for certainty, whereas lower fear would allow for the luxury of uncertainty? And, even further, would these differences mirror different ingrained experiences of living?

One intriguing area of study related to these questions has focused on people's differences in political attitudes and behaviors.

In this regard several findings have suggested both psychological and neurophysiological differences between liberals and conservatives (Azarain, 2016).   Four issues have been studied.

The first issue is that conservatives tend to focus on the negative. Dodd, et al. (2012) stated:

> Specifically, we find that greater orientation to aversive stimuli tends to be associated with right-of-center and greater orientation to appetitive (pleasing) stimuli with left-of-center political inclination.

These authors go on to point out that "though individual emotions clearly have unique neural and physiological characteristics," they tend to be organized into a biphasic system of aversive and appetitive motivational systems (Ibid.).

Furthermore:

Whatever the source of these biological and psychological predispositions, people may accordingly self-select, often sub-consciously, into situations likely to match their physiological and cognitive biases, according to the approach-avoidant spectrum. For example, those whose physiology responds strongly to violations of their preferences for protection, purity and order and are known to devote high levels of attention to such violations, are likely to take steps in their personal lives to avoid situations in which they encounter violations of security, purity and order. In other words, these individuals may be more likely to display the personal values of tradition, conformity and security. On the other hand, those whose physiology responds strongly to stimuli portraying desirable situations and experiences, and/or those who devote relatively high levels of attention to appetitive stimuli may be more likely to subscribe to the personal values of hedonism, stimulation and self-direction.

This suggests those on the political right are more attuned to what is aversive in life. Such an orientation is directly related to concerns about out-group threats and in-group norm violations. Those on the political left, less preoccupied with such concerns, are able to devote more attention to exploration, stimulation, and self-direction.

The second issue mentioned by Azarain (Ibid) is that conservatives have a stronger physiological response to threat—a "hypersensitivity to threat."

Said Azarain:

> One social psychologist from the University of Central Arkansas, Paul Nail, has a pretty interesting answer: "Conservatism, apparently, helps to protect people against some of the natural difficulties of living. The fact is we don't live in a completely safe world. Things can and do go wrong. But if I can impose this order on it by my worldview, I can keep my anxiety to a manageable level." This could explain the two parties' different stances on gun control. It only makes sense that those who startle more easily are also the ones that believe they need to own a gun.

The third issue mentioned by Azarain (Ibid) is that conservatives tend to fear new and different experiences. In a study of conservative and liberal students, researchers found differences in the items found in their bedrooms:

> ...while liberals owned more books and travel-related items, conservatives had more things that kept order in their lives, like calendars and cleaning supplies. This tells us

that liberals more often seek adventure and novel experiences. Conservatives, on the other hand, seem to prefer a more ordered, disciplined lifestyle. This could help explain why they are so resistant to change and progressive policies (Ibid, see also Laber-Warren, 2012).

This finding echoes studies using the Openness to New Experience Scale of the Five Factor Model of Personality (See BFI). The dimension of openness to new experience includes the following areas: ideas (curiosity), fantasy (imagination), aesthetics (being artistic), actions (having wide interests), feelings (being excitable), and values (being unconventional). High scorers are more open, whereas low scorers are more closed. High scorers are also more often liberal, and low scorers are more often conservative.

The fourth issue mentioned by Azarain (Ibid) is that conservative's brains are more reactive to fear.

Using MRI, scientists from University College London have found that students who identify themselves as conservatives have a larger amygdala than self-described liberals. This brain structure is involved in emotion processing and is especially reactive to fearful stimuli. It is possible that an oversized amygdala could create a heightened sensitivity that may cause one to habitually overreact to anything that appears to be a potential threat, whether it actually is one or not.

Such research suggests conservative and liberal people don't just have different options. They also have different brains. This, in turn, suggests lives that have adapted to different contexts—different sides of the fence as Frost would say.

In the London study cited above, Kanai, et al (Ibid) reported:

> Substantial differences exist in the cognitive styles of liberals and conservatives on psychological measures. Variability in political attitudes reflects genetic influences and their interaction with environmental factors. Recent work has shown a correlation between liberalism and conflict-related activity measured by event-related potentials originating in the anterior cingulate cortex. Here we show that this functional correlate of political attitudes has a counterpart in brain structure. In a large sample of young adults, we related self-reported political attitudes to gray matter volume using structural MRI. We found that greater liberalism was associated with increased gray matter volume in the anterior cingulate cortex, whereas greater conservatism was associated with increased

volume of the right amygdala. These results were replicated in an independent sample of additional participants. Our findings extend previous observations that political attitudes reflect differences in self-regulatory conflict monitoring and recognition of emotional faces by showing that such attitudes are reflected in human brain structure.

Thus, the anterior cingulate gyrus, which is associated with processing information in relation to decision making and choices, is a different, and higher order, structure than the right amygdala, which is associated with emotional processing, especially fear-based information.

These results suggest children raised in a climate of fear develop more conservative like-traits, whereas children raised in a more nurturing environment develop more liberal-like traits.

Such structural differences alone are able to predict liberal and conservative positions with 71.6 percent accuracy. It is not a big leap to think such differences are reflective of childhood environments.

Furthermore, predicting whether one is conservative or liberal based on his or her parents' positions yields a correlation of 69.5 percent.

"Not quite as good. And why is that interesting? It's because the brain is plastic, (Saltz see Rosenmann, 2016)."

"The brain is plastic and ever-changing, particularly in youth. ... Thinking certain thoughts or predominantly, let's say, utilizing your right amygdala versus your anterior cingulate gyrus inform the growth of those areas and therefore helps you predict later who is liberal and who is conservative," explained Saltz (Ibid).

Conservatives have been found to score higher in terms of stability, loyalty, not liking change, and incorporating religion. Liberals, on the other hand, have been found to like change, new information, and new experience. Such differences, it must be stressed, are not black or white, one or the other, in nature. Human traits, these included, tend to reflect a normal distribution (bell shaped curve) where differences appear on a gradient.

Feelings of threat and safety clearly are not constant over time. Laber-Warren (Ibid) argued:

Anxiety is an emotion that waxes and wanes in all of us, and as it swings up or down our political views can shift in its wake. When people feel safe and secure, they become more liberal; when they feel threatened, they become more conservative.

Such an effect was shown by Bargh (2017). Here, conservative Republicans were asked to imagine they possessed superpowers and were impermeable to injury. This mindset resulted in them making more liberal choices.

Another experiment was reported by Jost (2006). This concerned the topic of climate change:

> [In this study, we] reframed climate change not as a challenge to government and industry but as "a threat to the American way of life." After reading a passage that couched environmental action as patriotic, study participants who displayed traits typical of conservatives were much more likely to sign petitions about preventing oil spills and protecting the Arctic National Wildlife Refuge.

These results clearly reflect the importance of the context, in this case how the petitions were worded.

Healy (2017) reported:

> "There are a lot of citizens who are especially vigilant about potential threats

but not especially motivated or prepared to process information in a critical, systematic manner," said John Jost, co-director of New York University's Center for Social and Political Behavior. For years, Jost said, those Americans "have been presented with terrifying messages that are short on reason and openly contemptuous of scholarly and scientific standards of evidence."

Jost…said the new findings suggest that when dark claims and apocalyptic visions swirl, many of these anxious voters will cast skepticism aside and selectively embrace fearful claims, regardless of whether they're true (Ibid).

This suggests conservatives simply think differently. Such persons "show a lower tolerance for risk and have a greater need for closure and certainty, on average (Ibid)."

The above findings echo those of Lakoff (2009, 2016) who said:

Deeply embedded in conservative and liberal politics are two different models of the family. Conservatism is based on a Strict Father model, while liberalism is centered on a Nurturant Parent model. These two models of the family give rise to different moral systems.

The strict father is authoritarian. The nurturant parent tends to be liberal. Authoritarianism may be measured by the Authoritarianism Scale (see Scale). Here:

Right-wing authoritarians want society and social interactions structured in ways that increase uniformity and minimize diversity. In order to achieve that, they tend to be in favor of social control, coercion, and the use of group authority to place constraints on the behaviors of people such as political dissidents and ethnic minorities. These constraints might include restrictions on immigration, limits on free speech and association and laws regulating moral behavior. It is the willingness to support or take action that leads to increased social uniformity that makes right-wing authoritarianism more than just a personal distaste for difference. Right-wing authoritarianism is characterized by obedience to authority, moral absolutism, racial and ethnic prejudice, and intolerance and punitiveness towards dissidents and deviants. In parenting, right-wing authoritarians value children's obedience, neatness, and good manners.

The Authoritarian Scale (Altemeyer, 1981) asks people to choose between pairs of characteristics. Such pairs of characteristics include the following: independence or respect for elders, curiosity or good manners, self-reliance or obedience, and being considerate or well-behaved. Choosing: respect for elders, good manners, obedience, and being well behaved raises authoritarian scores.

It may be said there are "colliding differences" between those who score high on authoritarianism and those who score low. Such differences reflect the conservative-liberal divide.

Johnston (2018, see Edsall, 2018) wrote:

> Over the last few decades, party allegiances have become increasingly tied to a core dimension of personality we call "openness." Citizens high in openness value independence, self-direction, and novelty, while those low in openness value social cohesion, certainty, and security. Individual differences in openness seem to underpin many social and cultural disputes, including debates over the value of racial, ethnic, and cultural diversity, law and order, and traditional values and social norms.

People high in openness are more likely to be liberals, whereas people low in openness are more likely to be conservative. Those low in openness tend to have a fixed worldview as opposed to those who score high.   High scorers' views are much more fluid.

Hetherington (see Edsall, 2018) stated:

> The fixed tend to be wary of what they perceive as constant threats to their physical security specifically and of social change in general. The fluid are much more open to change and, indeed, see it as a strength. For them, anger lies in holding on to old ideas and rejecting diversity.

Further, people tend to divide into separate tribes according to these views.   Voting in favor of one's tribe may be more important than voting for issues.

Mason (2018) argued:

> The power behind the labels "liberal" and "conservative" to predict strong preferences for the ideological in-group is based largely in the social identification with those groups, not in the organization of attitudes associated with the labels. That is, even when we are discussing ideology — a presumably issue-based concept — we are not entirely discussing issues.

Stenner (2005) said:

> [My] universal theory [concerns] what causes intolerance of difference in general, which includes racism, political intolerance (e.g. restriction of free speech), moral intolerance (e.g. homophobia, supporting censorship, opposing abortion) and punitiveness. It demonstrates that all these seemingly disparate attitudes are principally caused by just two factors: individuals' innate psychological predispositions to intolerance ("authoritarianism") interacting with changing conditions of societal threat.

In this view, threatening conditions tend to increase authoritarian attitudes. Seen this way, people don't care about a given policy as much as they care about the "groups and symbols" with which a policy is associated.

Mason (Ibid.) stated:

> The results presented here suggest that political thought, behavior, and emotion are powerfully driven by political identities. The strength of a person's identification with his or her party affects how biased, active, and angry that person is, even if that person's issue positions are moderate.

If one's own group is held to be the only faction that understands what is truly happening, the collective projection of that group is held to be reality. Contradicting perceptions are routinely rejected.

This tends to be a self-maintaining position. Forsetti (2018), who grew up in white rural Christian America, claimed:

> In deep-red America, the white Christian god is king, figuratively and literally. Religious fundamentalism has shaped most of their [sic] belief systems. Systems built on a fundamentalist framework are not conducive to introspection, questioning, learning, or change. When you have a belief system built on fundamentalism, it isn't open to outside criticism, especially by anyone not a member of your tribe and in a position of power. The problem isn't that coastal elites don't understand rural Americans. The problem is that rural America doesn't understand itself and will *never* listen to anyone outside its bubble. It doesn't matter how "understanding" you are, how well you listen, what language you use...if you are viewed as an outsider, your views will be automatically discounted. I've had hundreds of discussions with rural white Americans and whenever I present them any information that contradicts their entrenched beliefs, no

matter how sound, how unquestionable, how obvious, they will not even entertain the possibility that it might be true. Their refusal is a result of the nature of their fundamentalist belief system and the fact that I'm the enemy because I'm an educated liberal.

Forsetti may be seen to be describing a closed system. External views are to be avoided.

...to them education is not to be trusted. Education is the enemy of fundamentalism because fundamentalism, by its very nature, is not built on facts. The fundamentalists I grew up around aren't anti-education. They want their kids to know how to read and write. They are against quality, in-depth, broad, specialized education. Learning is only valued up to a certain point. Once it reaches the level where what you learn contradicts doctrine and fundamentalist arguments, it becomes dangerous.

The result is a group that is not used to change. Furthermore, change typically only comes from within, and then primarily from persons who are held to be in authority. It is also for this reason that propaganda is so effective with such groups. Lacking critical reasoning skills, openness to new evidence, and a willingness to re-evaluate positions, the group is largely unable to adequately evaluate information.

When a child is afraid of the dark, it is possible to comfort him or her. This is the case, because the child trusts you and will listen to what you say. But, says Forsetti: "When someone doesn't trust you and isn't open to anything not already accepted as true in their [sic] belief system, there really isn't much, if anything, you can do."

Forsetti (Ibid.) felt that what *was* capable of changing views of fundamentalist authoritarians was an experience that had become "intensely personal." For example, hatred of gay people could sometimes be modified if a loved member of one's family came out. Still, this may not be enough.

> What I understand is that rural Christian white Americans are entrenched in fundamentalist belief systems; don't trust people outside their tribe; have been force-fed a diet of misinformation and lies for decades; are unwilling to understand their own situations; and truly believe whites are superior to all races (Ibid.).

The fear behind such positions is not insignificant. And this fear is perpetuated from parent to child, generation to generation. Further, such persons are poorly suited to life outside the system and the very different ways in which such a life operates. Teaching children to be afraid of any disobedience tends to position them for lives of fearful servitude. This is clearly not the way to develop a strong society.

Appeals to God to justify such training are psychologically damaging—plain and simple.

Adaptability is essential for both mental health and social progress. Learning how to function in the world we actually have maximizes capability. On the contrary, cleaving to a group that is insular and rejecting of reason and new information minimizes adaptability in all but focused areas. This is not merely a debate between political parties or points of view. It involves questions of how a culture best tries to advance into a multi-dimensional and multi-national world it actually inhabits. Helping the child learn his or her dark fears are irrational *helps* the child. And while fear is a natural state, fear of everything is not. If all of life is seen as dangerous, psychological intervention is necessary.

The fences need to come down.

REFERENCES

Azarian, B.   Fear and Anxiety Drive Conservatives' Political Attitudes. Psychology Today, 12-16.

Bargh, J.   At Yale, We Conducted an Experiment to Turn Conservatives into Liberals.   The Results Say a Lot About Our Political Divisions. The Washington Post, 11-22-17.

BFI.   http://fetzer.org/sites/default/files/images/stories/pdf/selfmeasures/Personality-BigFiveInventory.pdf

Dodd, M.D., Balzer, A., Jacobs, C.M., Gruszczynski, M.W. Smith, K. B., and Hibbing, J.R.   The Political Left Rolls with the Good and the Political Right Confronts the Bad: Connecting Physiology and Cognition to Preferences. http://rstb.royalsocietypublishing.org/content/367/1589/640.full#aff-1

Edsall, T.B.   The Contract with Authoritarianism.   New York Times, 04-05-18.

Forsetti. An Insider Explains How Rural White Christian America Has A Dark And Terrifying Underbelly.   Raw Story.   02-06-18.

Frost, R.   Mending Wall, Norton Anthology of Modern Poetry. Ellmann, R. and O'Clair, R. (Eds.). Norton, 1973, pp. 193-194.

Healy, M. Why Conservatives are More Likely than Liberals to Believe False Information about Threats. Los Angeles Times, 02-02-17.

Jost, J.T. The End of the End of Ideology. American Psychologist, Vol 61, No. 7, 10-06, pp. 651-670.

Kanai, R., Feilden, T., Firth, C., and Rees, G. Political Orientations are Correlated with Brain Structure in Young Adults. Current Biology, Vol 8., 04-26-11, pp 677-680. https://www.ncbi.nlm.nih.gov/pmc/articles/PMC3092984/#bib1

Laber-Warren, E. Unconscious Reactions separate Liberals and Conservatives. Scientific American. 09-12.

Lakoff, G. Moral Politics: How Liberals and Conservatives Think. Third Edition. Chicago, 2016.

Lakoff, G. The Political Mind: A Cognitive Scientist's Guide to Your Brain and its Politics. Penguin. Reprint Edition. 2009.

Mason, L. Ideologues Without Issues: the Polarizing Consequences of Ideological Identities. Public Opinion Quarterly. 03-21-18.

Rosenmann, A. Study: Liberals and Conservatives have Different Brain Structures. Salon. 06-16.

Scale. https://openpsychometrics.org/tests/RWAS/

Stenner, K. The Authoritarian Dynamic. Cambridge. 2005.

NARCISSISM: CULTURE

There likely has not been a time when culture was not in flux. Certainly, flux appears to have increased in frequency. In our time there seems to be a gap between each one of us as fracture lines separate old people from young, rich from poor, male from female, East Coast from West Coast, educated from non-educated, religious from non-religious, race one from race two, sick from well, &c., among others.

Such distinctions have always existed, yet they appear to be growing cavernous. It could be argued we have become a society of polarities. Increasingly we each have our in-group media—which opposes out-group media. We have our own people with our own attitudes. We rarely listen to each other.

Much of the reason for this development has been laid at the feet of the internet. It is that device that has allowed for radical segregation. Increasingly we are plugged into our devices instead of interacting directly with each other. Our devices are plugged into sectors we favor, even within the same family. We get our contacts from them. We get our own subset of the news from them. We get our particular entertainment from them. We buy things on them. All of this can be conducted without our having to go anywhere.

There are entire universes of sites that cater to people like we are. Other universes cater to others. It can be non-stop. Morning to night we are able to tune in—everywhere we go —to what we want. We are equally able to avoid what we don't want. Such a practice leads us to islands of experience.

Earlier cultures had to deal with the demise of the ve. Villages were arranged around a common area meant to be shared by all. There people could meet, play, rest, run a few sheep, and keep in contact with their neighbors. What doomed the commons was greed. One person began running too many sheep and thereby profiting excessively. Neighbors noticed and began running more sheep themselves. Soon there was no more commons.

A similar sort of greed is at work in our own commons. Voices seek to out-shout other voices. It becomes a cacophony. The more voices, the more volume is required in order to be heard and thus to have more clout. But which voices are these?

In *The Genealogy of Morals* Nietzsche wrote that the majority of the culture defines ethics and principles that favor itself. Think of a best-fit line through the average of the culture. As long as one behaves in line with the average, the culture approves of him or her. Problems arise for those who are deviant, either too far above the norm or too far below.

This creates a problem for the superior person (Ubermensch). Being superior to the culture, the superior person is able to use his or her abilities to aid the culture, *but* this must be accomplished in a tolerably disguised fashion, so the normative culture does not retaliate against the superior person for being deviant.

It is a bit like being a spy and not knowing who can be trusted and who cannot—so one ends up trusting no one.

Cultures attempt to protect themselves, so they can survive. In order to do this, there has to be a restriction of empathy to members of the group. Outsiders are to be avoided or battled (see Campbell, 1988, Eliade, 1963). This is a procedure that is designed to promote the integrity and survival of the group.

When a culture becomes as splintered and polarized as ours has become, one must be on guard to protect the group from almost everyone around. The commons have become filled with insular groups seeking to flourish. In an overall sense, there is no longer an *us*. There is a *many of us*. And we are opposed to each other.

Divisions of groups tend to form along fracture lines of the culture. Additional sub-groups also form. Adherence to one group may or may not preclude interest and/or involvement in another. Thinking goes from highly flexible to highly black and white. This occurs in all groups at all levels.

When thinking moves toward a black and white position, compromise becomes increasingly impossible. Empathic understanding ceases. Power becomes the unit of trade.

Psychologically, one of the reasons this happens is that we tend to identify with our positions. Like our possessions, they are part of who we are. They may be a large part. Thus, it isn't just our position that is at stake, it is our identity. If your identity wins out, it means mine is inferior. It may also mean my entire group is inferior, my parents, my friends, and my loved ones.

This is the precise dilemma that was faced by the Buddha: the tie to lust and fear. These, he held, must be overcome in order to come to peace (see Hanh, 1999). Such a thing was accomplished, he realized, by not attaching one's worth to the having of power or things. Christian monks have held similar positions.

But if we let go of power and things, others will take them and be in charge of the culture. They will determine how affairs will go.

The issue for the Buddha was not culture, but peace. Wars, on the other hand, are fought for control of cultures —for control of what the culture *has*, who can *control* the culture.

The one with power must defend that power or lose it. We have developed laws to protect our things and our extreme behavior. Both of these tend to reduce our openness to each other.   Instead, we seek to advance beyond each other.

Soon, in our pursuit of power and things, we tend to lose track of what it is to be a human being. What *is* it to be a human being *before* one becomes consciously an adherent to a group? Answering this question may not be easy.

All of us are born into a group of some sort. We are born in one place or another, one culture or another, one or another racial group, &c. Our parents are members of a group. Their friends are. One's schools are in this place instead of that place.

Further, people are either interested in other groups, or they are only interested in their own. They seek knowledge and experiences beyond their group, or they do not. I am encouraged to be like them. I may be punished if I am not like them.

My people may be convinced their views are *correct*. They may instead believe their views are *one* of many possible views. These are attitudes and beliefs I will internalize as part of the group. My parents may haul me around the world. They may never leave home.

A teenage peer group may be seen as a subculture that exists to facilitate separation from the parental group. Though this subculture is constantly moving, it always stands in opposition to the parental group. It is, if you will, one's first taste of being an adult.

Some of us abandon our parents as much as possible and attempt to completely dissolve into the peer group. Some of us avoid the peer group and stick closely to our parents. Some of us attempt to have one foot on the shore and another in the boat. Which position we take says much about what the assumptions were surrounding us in our childhoods.

Wealth and power are highly esteemed in our culture. Sometimes other things are valued as well: education, kindness, innovation (thinking), &c.

Twentieth century developments in philosophy illustrated the connection between where one stands and what one sees (Foucault (1994), Heidegger (see Richardson, 2012), Gadamer (1977), Wittgenstein (1953), et al.) The same thing seen from a different perspective will appear differently. Thus, the context in which a thing is seen as well as the thing seen exist *together* as a unit of perception.

This logic applies to groups. The, say, far right doesn't look the same from the far right as it looks from the far left. Nor is it the case that one must have cancer before one can understand it. Views differ. It is the nature of views.

The above considerations become strained when there is tyranny. Here one group dominates and excludes another. We may say only one color is legal. Tyranny is an example of power run amuck at the expense of truth and humanity. This can be seen insomuch as the truth is not as important as the tyrannical position, and empathy is discouraged in order to strengthen the tyranny.

Tyranny is a tragedy. The destruction of truth and humanity is the opposite of human development. Power need not have any quality except itself. This is so destructive, because it erases individual voices.

The first thing an invading force tries to accomplish is to knock out the media. Then no one will be able to know what is going on. Without a voice one cannot know who one is. One gets lost. We are profoundly social creatures, and it is vital our thoughts and options can be responded to by others.

Seen in this sense, the most advanced culture is the one that maximally allows all voices to be heard. Not just the powerful. All voices. When all voices matter, all persons matter. Widening the circle to include as many voices as possible is a different project from the one we have often pursued.

Allowing all voices to be heard must wait a culture in which people are not afraid of diverse input. This requires a degree of maturity as a person. I must understand I have a view, and so do you. I may think your view is silly or wrong, and you may think that about mine. But we have to allow each other to speak, and we have to try to have some understanding of what each other says.

Cultures and subcultures that become intolerant avoid hearing any but their own voices. Often these cultures seek to silence other voices. Other voices are devalued or condemned. This becomes a culture not *among* others but *against* others. It is a culture by *imposition* as opposed to a culture that develops *organically*.

Such a culture is inherently weak. It relies on power and intimidation to survive. It may be seen as the maximization of lust and fear. It is a culture that is by its very nature surrounded. The history of the world is littered by such cultures that have risen, flourished, and fallen.

What destroys them? A voice. An alternate voice. Something they are not.

The framers of the American constitution conceived of a culture that would exist in a tension of differing views. This was thought to be a bulwark against the sort of tyranny these people had experienced in England and Europe. Voices would compete. A form of worked-out compromise would prevail.

Such an ideal has not been easy to enact. From the start factions have been loathe to compromise (Russell, 2010). During the U.S. Civil War, the country even went to war against itself. This was a war over the claimed right of certain people to own and exploit other people.

Power bestows advantages it may be practically impossible to resist. Those with power want to preserve their positions—sometimes at any cost. Power equals the ability to position oneself over others. Often this is far from benign. It may be, in fact, impossible to have a culture other than one of haves and have-nots.

In a sense power works as the opposite of inclusion. It is power that determines what can and cannot be heard. By definition this leads to an imbalance in the culture. It becomes lop-sided.   Unapproved views are forced underground. Strife and resentment build.

In order to maintain power such effects must not bother one. Everything must be sacrificed in the service of power itself. Huge empires have been defended with the blood of the children of those who have no voice.

The concept of collective narcissism may be applied in this case.   This concept applies to the application of narcissistic traits to social groups.   The group behaves narcissistically, and individual's selves are based on the group identity instead of an individual one.

> ...the concept of collective narcissism [is] an emotional investment in an unrealistic belief about the in-group's greatness – aiming to explain how feelings about an in-group shape a tendency to aggress against out-groups. The results of 5 studies indicate that collective, but not individual, narcissism predicts inter-group aggressiveness. Collective narcissism is related to high private and low public collective self-esteem and low implicit group esteem. It predicts perceived threat from out-groups, unwillingness to forgive out-groups and preference for military aggression over and above social dominance orientation, right wing authoritarianism, and blind patriotism. The relationship between collective

narcissism and aggressiveness is mediated by perceived threat from out-groups and perceived insult to the in-group. In sum, the results indicate that collective narcissism is a form of high but ambivalent group esteem related to sensitivity to threats to the in-group's image and retaliatory aggression (Golec de Zavala, et al. 2009).

Collective narcissism is thus a practice of identification with important social groups in a narcissistic way.

Collective narcissists may see groups as extensions of themselves and expect everybody to recognize not only their individual greatness but also the prominence of their in-groups. It has also been suggested that especially in collectivistic cultures individual narcissism may stem from the reputation and honor of the groups to which one belongs (Ibid.)

Identification with a group may also occur when individuals feel they must protect a weak and threatened ego (Adorno, 1998).

...narcissistic identification with an in-group is likely to emerge in social and cultural contexts that diminish the ego and/or socialize individuals to put their [sub]group in the centre of their lives, attention, emotions and actions. Thus, the development of narcissistic group identification can be fostered by certain social contexts independently of individual-level narcissism (Ibid).

An aggressive and defensive stance is common against out-groupers.

Interpersonal aggression is a means of defending the grandiose self-image. Narcissists invest emotionally in their high opinion of themselves, demand that others confirm that opinion and punish those who seem unlikely to do so. Since they require constant validation of unrealistic greatness of the self, narcissists are likely to continually encounter threats to their self-image and be chronically intolerant of them (Ibid.)

Collective narcissism has to do with how the group is valued by others.

Collective narcissists are determined to get the recognition of others. When they think their group is not sufficiently recognized, they advocate hostile revenge. They attack not only the 'offenders' but the whole groups they represent. In our studies, when their group was criticized by one person, collective narcissists responded with aggressive intentions and behaviours (sic) towards the whole group (**Ibid.**).

Collective narcissists are also indirectly hostile. They rejoice in misfortunes of groups or people they hold accountable for offending their group (see also Goldsmith).

Heightened acuity routinely gives rise to conspiracy theories directed against the group.

Kohut (1984) outlined the role narcissistic structure plays in power situations. As a result of non-empathic parenting, he said, the child develops an inadequate sense of self. But instead of admitting this inadequate self (which would require an adequate self), the child adopts the *guise* of an adequate self. The true self—the inadequate self—is eclipsed by the guise self—the adequate self.

In other words, one pretends to be who one is not. The pretend self is cast as the opposite of the real self: it is capable, confident, and deserving of all rewards.

Other people who respond favorably to this pretend self are approved of by the narcissistic person. Those who refuse to go along with the pretend self and, rather, respond to the real self are considered threats.

Real damage can occur when narcissistic individuals get into power in organizations. A "yes-man" culture is routinely established. Those who gratify the narcissist are promoted. Those who can't bear this requirement are let go. Here the emphasis is shifted from work production to the project of gratifying the narcissistic leader.

It is of vital importance that the narcissistic person work to keep his or her true (inadequate) self concealed behind the capable-appearing exterior. Input that is able to get through this defensive filter is extremely wounding. The result of such a wound is typically rage.

Mika (2017) argued:

> All tyrants share several essential features: they are predominantly men with a specific character defect, narcissistic psychopathology (a.k.a. malignant narcissism). This defect manifests in a severely impaired or absent conscience and an insatiable drive for power and adulation that masks the conscience deficits. It forms the core of attraction between him and his followers, the essence of what is seen as his "charisma" (p. 299).

The need to be considered special or better than others can become a consuming passion. Nothing is allowed to stand in its way.

The logic is similar to Hegel's master-slave distinction:

> ...the only alternative to being an object (slave) for the other is to become a subject (master) for whom the other is an object (slave) (Mollon, 1993, p. 27, see also Benjamin, 1988).

Thus, a struggle ensues to determine who is going to be the master and who the slave. It is important for the narcissistic person to appear superior in all things precisely because this protects him from facing his own shameful feelings of inadequacy.

Entire segments of a culture may be narcissistic. That is, as in the case of racism, one segment may have a profound need to appear superior to another segment. The culture itself may conceive of one segment as superior. Such superiority may be used to excuse all manner of unfairness, denial, and cruelty. Nations, as well, may be narcissistic.

Love (2016) wrote in terms of the Trump administration:

> I think it's time to take a good look in the mirror: Is there any better symbol of what's gone wrong in mainstream American culture than a greedy, superficial, sociopathic megalomaniac reality TV star who makes constant displays of fragile and toxic masculinity? These are the qualities we, as a

culture, too often celebrate and encourage. Money and fame are our core values. Success at any price. Cut-throat business practices. Bullshit your way to the top (see Love).

Also:

Finally, at a time when most (white) Americans are safer than they've ever been, we've culturally adjusted to a constant climate of fear. Fear of the other: gays, blacks, Muslims, Mexicans, Russians, Chinese, terrorists, people coming to take our guns. Our news channels endlessly broadcast the new threats we must live in fear of and our TV programs teach us survival skills for the upcoming apocalypse, putting our collective survival down (once again) to the individual. We make ever greater sacrifices of our principles, liberty and humanity in order to defend ourselves from these supposed threats. We become ever easier prey for those who seek to abuse those fears in their quest for power (Ibid).

Love argues that when we condemn such a situation, we are actually condemning ourselves. Talking about our own issues and problems is far harder than talking about the issues and problems of others.

These remarks are echoed by Tolentino (see Tolentino).

If you are strongly averse to something, won't you inevitably have trouble recognizing it within yourself? The religious fear of evil can itself lead to evil—a desire to protect unborn children, for instance, can cause a callous disregard for women's lives. The fear of being inconsistent about one's feminism often leads one to be inconsistent about one's feminism. Fixating on any demon necessitates a deep familiarity with it, and today my fear of narcissism derives from intimate acquaintance with the many evolving ways a person can bend her life into a flattering mirror online.

If "toxic self-absorption" is indeed the new American disease, then it will be important to remember that no one has immunity. The story of the narcissist is, in part, a story of the people around him pleading for empathy, insisting that we should all care more about one another. And yet somehow this account of the world has become "a story that divides us, by defining empathy as something we have and others lack," Dombek writes. Perhaps in pathologizing narcissism, we have forgotten how perilous it is to constantly diagnose other people. In the end, what "The Selfishness of Others" lays out most clearly is not the danger of narcissism but, rather, the danger of any particular world view that requires, for the sake of consistency, its owner to believe that she is good.

Remes (see Remes) cautions the assumption that narcissism is the explanation for every ill.

Narcissism lies on a continuum from healthy to pathological. Healthy narcissism is part of normal human functioning. It can represent healthy self-love and confidence that is based on real achievement, the ability to overcome setbacks and derive the support needed from social ties.

But narcissism becomes a problem when the individual becomes preoccupied with the self, needing excessive admiration and approval from others, while showing disregard for other people's sensitivities. If the narcissist does not receive the attention desired, substance abuse and major depressive disorder can develop.

Narcissists often portray an image of grandiosity or overconfidence to the world, but this is only to cover up deep feelings of insecurity and a fragile self-esteem that is easily bruised by the slightest criticism. Because of these traits, narcissists find themselves in shallow relationships that only serve to satisfy their constant need for attention. When narcissistic traits become so pronounced that they lead to impairment this can indicate the presence of narcissistic personality disorder.

The history of religion is rife with precisely this kind of phenomenon. The history of civilizations is not far behind.

In narcissistic construction the focus is on the self and its worth. Each self is considered to be on its own, vying to see who is on top.

According to McWilliams (1994):

What narcissistic people of all appearances have in common is an inner sense of, and/or terror of, insufficiency, shame, weakness, and inferiority. Their compensatory behaviors might diverge greatly yet still reveal similar preoccupations (p. 171).

Such persons, we may assume, are too busy trying to deal with their own hidden feelings of inadequacy to be able to put energy into helping the group become more healthy and beneficial to everyone. As detailed above, the group itself becomes a narcissistic entity struggling for adequacy against other groups.

This situation is very dangerous. When groups polarize against each other, the sense of a common reality gets lost. Society begins to resemble rival high school athletic teams: first one side wins and then the other. The winning side takes all the spoils and delights in leaving as little as possible to the losers. Then the sides shift.

Bruck (2018) quoted Jerry Brown, the governor of California, as saying of recent American politics:

> ..." a cycle [can] be created, in which one side pushes as far as it can until it's thrown out, then the next one does it, and then it will happen again...So...the Democrats get more extreme, the Republicans get more extreme, and you have an ungovernable America. And a stop-start, not-reliable superpower. Other people will have to react to that level of uncertainty, and that will not be positive for America's role in the world (p. 47).

Extreme narcissism may be seen as a way to drop out of the collective and attempt to become an island to oneself. If it is all about us versus them, there is no we.

Recovery from a narcissistic context is not easy.

It is important to realize that in any culture there are narcissistic as well as non-narcissistic groups. The call to polarity is heard differently by different people. A more developed world view can see several sides of any issue and be comfortable with such diversity. More primitive world views are routinely polarized.

If the rival high school is okay with some wins and some losses as simply the way it is, a polarized school faces a different kind of opponent. Here, no matter who wins or loses, the result is considered to be an ordinary event in time. The groups' esteem does not depend on the outcome. The loser does not lose face, and the winner does not attain glory. It is simply a game.

In non-narcissistic contexts, in other words, value judgments are largely held at bay or are ostensibly absent. If one's inadequate self can emerge and *not* be judged as inadequate, one is able to experience a different sort of interaction than one has known.

The trick is allowing oneself to find a non-narcissistic context. In light of such a context, polarized contexts are able to appear as unenlightened and unhealthy. One can focus one's efforts on strengthening the non-narcissistic context in an effort to promote a less judgmental whole. Rogers (1989) called it unconditional positive regard. The other is worth while simply because he or she is a person. Admittance to the group does not have to be achieved by having the right views.

A culture that can hear itself is far healthier than one that cannot. The ability to hear oneself requires being able to get outside of, or beyond, oneself. It requires a new perspective.

REFERENCES

Adorno, T. Critical models: Interventions and Catchwords. New York: Columbia University Press 1998.

Benjamin, J. The Bonds of Love. Pantheon, 1988.

Bruck, C. California V. Trump: Jerry Brown's Attempt to Moderate a Radical White House. The New Yorker, 2018, pp. 36-47.

Campbell, J. The Power of Myth. Doubleday, 1988.

Campbell, J. The Inner Reaches of Outer Space: Metaphor as Myth and as Religion. Harper. 1986.

Eliade, M. Myth and Reality. Harper, 1963.

Foucault, M. The Order of Things: An Archeology of the Human Sciences. Vintage, 1994.

Gadamer, H-J. and Linge, D.E. Philosophical Hermeneutics. California, 1977

Goldsmith. https://goldsmithspsychologyblog.wordpress.com/2017/01/23/what-to-expect-when-collective-narcissists-get-political-power/

Golec de Zavala, Agnieszka and Cichocka, Aleksandra and Eidelson, Roy and Jayawickreme, Nuwan (2009) Collective

Narcissism and its Social Consequences. Journal of Personality and Social Psychology, 97 (6). pp. 1074-1096.

Hanh, T. N. The Heart of the Buddha's Teaching: Transforming Suffering into Peace, Joy, and Liberation. Broadway Books, 1999.

Kohut, H. How Does Analysis Cure? Chicago, 1984.

Love. https://www.alternet.org/election-2016/donald-trump-gives-america-good-look-mirror

McWilliams, N. Psychoanalytic Diagnosis: Understanding Personality Structure in the Clinical Process. Guilford, 1994.

Mika, E. Who Goes Trump? Tyranny as a Triumph of Narcissism. In Lee, B. (Ed.) The Dangerous Case of Donald Trump. St. Martin's, 2017, pp. 298 - 318.

Mollon, P. The Fragile Self: The Structure of Narcissistic Disturbance and its Therapy. Aronson, 1993.

Nietzsche, F. The Philosophy of Nietzsche. Modern Library, 1954.

Remes, O. http://theconversation.com/why-are-we-becoming-so-narcissistic-here's-the-science-55773

Richardson, J. Heidegger. Routledge, 2012.

Rogers, C. The Carl Rogers Reader. Mariner, 1989.

Russell, T. A Renegade History of the United States. Free Press, 2010.

Tolentino, J. https://www.newyorker.com/culture/jia-tolentino/what-happens-when-we-decide-everyone-else-is-a-narcissist

Wittgenstein, L. Philosophical Investigations. Macmillan, 1953.

NARCISSISM: DOA—DELUSIONS OF ADEQUACY

In the Japanese art of war, it is thought wise to lay siege to the castle but not quite conquer it. This leaves the castle weakened after spending its arms and energy on the siege, but it also requires the troops of the castle to remain in place to defend it. The invaders, meanwhile, are free to reposition themselves in many different configurations as they seek advantage.

This is a difference between being required to stay in one spot and defend one's turf versus being free to move around to gain options.

The castle may serve as a metaphor for the narcissistic experience.

The narcissistic experience is one of having to maintain a (superior) appearance behind which one can conceal one's (inferior) reality.

There is a fundamental difference between what is real and the appearance of what is real. In any particular situation, however, it may be difficult to tell which is which. This is true as appearance is modeled on what is real. That is, to be useful, the appearance must closely resemble the real. That is how one learns how to do it.

The whole enterprise is helped or hindered depending on whether one has parents who were themselves real or has parents who operated in terms of appearances. That is, in one case the base upon which family interactions take place is reality—or the base upon which family interactions take place is appearance.

The rules in these different families will also tend to be different. In the real family, reality will be valued more highly than appearance. The real is what will be actively sought. In the appearance family, reality will be shunned in favor of appearance. The two may be contradictory.

In either family what is practiced over and over is what becomes proficiently done. Children raised in real families are routinely not highly practiced in appearance. Children raised in appearance families are not routinely highly practiced at being real.

This is akin to the advantage of having a natural language or a mother tongue (*Mutter Sprache*). Wittgenstein (1953) held that native speakers of a language were the experts in that language. They know how to do it. Someone learning the language can learn from a native speaker.

Similarly, being real or relying on appearance become natural abilities. As Jung (1964) showed, as one trait is emphasized, others become weaker. One who spends all his or her days reading is different sort of person in ability from one who spends all his or her days running.

As a rule, we do what we are good at doing, and we avoid what we are bad at doing. Our strength gets stronger, and our lack gets weaker.

Then we all show up at school. There we, with our numerous different backgrounds, try to fit together. It is not an easy task. Some of us are used to interacting with people who are different; some of us are not. Some of us have a natural ability; some of us less so.

Our task is to start at the beginning and slowly develop more complex abilities. It is vital we are supported in this project as persons of worth simply for being who we are. This is the case as we need to feel we are okay even though we are not yet very able.

If we are adequately supported, we won't have to worry about our worth while we learn our tasks. We will be able to fully focus on the tasks. If, on the other hand, we are not adequately supported we will have to manage our struggling sense of worth while, at the same time, we try to attend to our tasks (see Kohut, 1984).

Attempting to do two things at once doubles the demands on our resources. We may begin to fall behind. There are (at least) two ways we can try to come to grips with this situation: 1) try harder to accomplish the task, or 2) *pretend* to be able to do the task. This latter option allows us to somewhat rescue our sagging sense of worth and, at the same time, appear to be as capable as our peers.

The problem with the pretend-option is that one's real ability remains poor at the same time one's appearance seems adequate. This will require an additional task. I will have to *hide* the truth of my actual ability behind my appearance. If anyone were to find out the truth of my poor ability I would feel humiliated and ashamed.

An enormous difficulty with trying to be real is that improvements in one's real ability take time. Sometimes it is plodding work. It takes far less time to pretend competence—and the pretense will work in many instances.

In college there were students who bragged that they never studied. The implication was that they were so bright things came quickly to them. Others plodded along, feeling stupid, and trying to improve their abilities.

Certainly, there are those who seem to "get it" more quickly or "grasp the thread" more readily than others. Some have a natural affinity for certain subjects (e.g. abstract reasoning). Nonetheless in many cases building one's ability is like building a house—solidly made foundations are an asset.

The problem intensifies if the appearance group begins to shine more brightly than the real group. The appearance of super intelligence, unusual prowess, outstanding capacity, &c. shine ever more brightly. Soon the real group can seem pedestrian compared to the éclat of the appearance group.

It can be said the effective skill is different in these two groups. The goal for the real group is integrity. The goal for the appearance group is the hiding of its real condition as well as a search for acclaim.

I spoke (above) to the importance of *support* for one's worth as one was learning and developing.

Parents and teachers differ in terms of what they support. On the one hand, parents and teachers may support *who* the child is—*whoever* he or she is. On the other hand, parents and teachers may support *what* the child is able to do. Here the more achievement, the more support.

The difference is between a child who feels of worth for *who* he or she is versus a child who feels of worth in terms of what he or she is able to *do*. In this latter case, the worth is *contingent* on what is accomplished.

Clearly it is more difficult to plod along, trying to learn the nuts and bolts of topics, than it is to display prowess whether or not one has it—or to which degree one has it.

In the midst of information overload, it is often difficult to slow down enough to genuinely learn anything really well. Data and facts may be presented at such speed it is very difficult, if not impossible, to deeply understand them. In this situation, one finds oneself learning a little about a good number of things—but knowing none of them in any depth.

There is both a plus and a minus to this situation. On the one hand studies in postmodernism and linguistic philosophy have taught us about the dangers of having a limited point of view. Since things appear different from different contexts, it is important to experience several contexts in order to learn how those different contexts influence what is being seen.

On the other hand, one's knowledge of different data and facts can be broad but shallow. Thus, one may be aware of a great number of things, but not know any of them very well. In this case one's knowledge tends to be dilettantish.

Optimal development requires a positive and accepting exchange between a parent and a child. If the parent is not experienced as positive—or is experienced ambivalently— the child will have trouble developing a positive sense of self (Fonagy, 2001).

Such a child will seek external approval to shore up his or her own self esteem. If achievement or external approval fails, the child will likely experience strong feelings of worthlessness, depression, and anger (narcissistic rage). This anger is routinely directed toward others who the child feels have let him down.

The above issues become more complicated by the addition of power. One view may rise in power against other views and prevail. Power, thus, may dictate what is heard and what is not heard. Further, power tends to work toward its own preservation.

There is a tendency for groups to strive for survival and well-being. This can pit groups against each other.

Primitive cultures strove to strengthen the group against outsiders (Eliad, 1963).

Depending on the stability and health of the group, different viewpoints may or may not be tolerated. Deficiency arises when the efforts of the group to protect itself restricts or outlaws new and different input. In this case the group has positioned itself against its own ability to learn and develop.

This is how groups may appear either open or closed. Open groups tend to focus on what is exterior to them, whereas closed groups tend to focus on themselves.

In terms of society as a whole it is significant whether the group or groups in power tend to be open or closed. It is also significant whether the group or groups in power tend to be based on reality or appearance.

In this light it is important to consider the history of tyranny. Mika (2017) has outlined the development of a pathological process in relation to power. She argued that narcissism was the essential element in this process.

Mika (Ibid) argued:

> Impulsive, sensation-seeking, and incapable of experiencing empathy or guilt, a narcissistic psychopath treats other people as objects of need fulfillment and wish fulfillment. This makes it easy for him to use and abuse them, in his personal relationships

and in large-scale actions, without compunction. His lack of conscience renders him blind to higher human values, which allows him to disregard them entirely or treat them instrumentally as means to his ends, the same way he treats people (p. 300).

This kind of constellation, however, may aid in the "pursuit of power, money, and adulation (Ibid.)."

Character traits that develop into narcissistic psychopathy are observable in the childhood of such persons. There is also, frequently, a history of childhood abuse.

Such persons appear rigid and narrow. They do not experience inner conflicts, so they create external ones. They are deficient in empathy, so they seek to control others (Ibid.).

Tyrants prosper when they find supporters who are aggrieved. Kimmel (see Rosin, 2013) spoke of "aggrieved entitlement." Such people have been hurt and feel entitled to revenge.

Such people readily identify with a narcissistic leader who projects a bigger than life persona. Such identification makes them feel as successful and as powerful as the leader instead of being the hurting failures they really are. That is to say, these followers hold to the appearance and avoid the reality.

Fromm (1980) said:

> The narcissism of the leader who is
> convinced of his greatness, and who has no
> doubts, is precisely what attracts the
> narcissism of those who submit to him (see
> Mika, Ibid, p. 306).

In this fashion the tyrant is given the task to avenge the
hurts and humiliations of the followers and punish those
who inflicted the hurts.

This process becomes lethal when a split is made between
ourselves versus those who have hurt us. Girard (1979,
1989) has pointed to the vital role of the scapegoat in the
development and maintenance of civilization. It is good for
group solidarity to have an enemy.

This operates in terms of the notion of alterity. Alterity is
thought to develop in three steps: 1) a distinction is made
between oneself and others. This allows oneself to be a
person, but reduces others to being a member of a class of
persons. 2) unwanted thoughts and feelings in the self are
projected onto the others. This means oneself is good,
whereas others are bad. 3) The process is institutionalized.

Mika (2017) said:

> The natural consequence of scapegoating that
> stems from the projections of the narcissist's

devalued parts of himself is dehumanization of the Others, which then justifies all kinds of atrocities perpetrated on them...Once we dehumanize the Others and imbue them with a murderous motivation directed at us [our own projection], we can easily rationalize any act of violence we perpetrate upon them as self-defense (pp. 308, 309).

This is an extreme case. The widespread lack of awareness of negative thoughts, emotions, and impulses, however, makes it difficult to tease out individual contributions to hostility and cruelty to others.

In more mild fashion, people can protect themselves from negative self-evaluations by limiting input. That is, if one's sense of adequacy means having no lack, one is in the "perfection predicament." Such a state is unachievable by human beings in reality.

The solution, often, is to appear all-wise, all-capable, and all-knowing. This renders one unable to learn new things, because one needs to appear all-capable already.

In order to appear on top of things, numerous people monopolize conversations, argue about virtually everything, and avoid cooperative conversations in order to convince others—and themselves—they are in charge.

This leads to the development of the authoritarian person who demands to be in charge. Such a person demands allegiance. Non-followers are denigrated or punished in order to maintain the authoritarian's sense of superiority. The world is split into those who are with me and those who are against me. The result is war.

Delusions of adequacy protect a fragile sense of self.

In order to develop a tolerably robust sense of self, one has to experience a positive and welcoming interaction with one's parent—or, in some cases, with another. This positive interaction is internalized and serves as a model of the self and of others. If the parent is experienced negatively—or ambivalently—the relationship with the child will suffer. What is then internalized is a negative sense of self and others.

The world is divided into those who are "with me" and those who are "against me." The task is no longer harmonious interactions, but competition and a wary attitude.

Few things increase the solidarity of a group like having an enemy. The endless battle between good and evil, where we define ourselves as the good guys and others as the bad guys has colored much human history.

Furthermore, it is easy to conflate power with what is good. To automatically assume oneself is the good guy without proof is grandiose. Also, to assume that since one is a parent, his or her thoughts and feelings therefore have more weight than the thoughts and feelings of a child requires a lack of empathy.

Malkin (2017) said:

> Pathological narcissism begins when people become so addicted to feeling special that, just like with any drug, they'll do anything to get their "high," including lie, steal, cheat, betray, and even *hurt* those closest to them (see Lee 2017, p. 57).

It is easy to see how a leader or a parent whose personality structure is based on an insecure attachment and who has developed an over-competent persona to hide secret vulnerabilities, fear, and sense of weakness must never appear to falter.

Malkin (Ibid) added:

> Exploitation and entitlement (or EE in the research) are linked to just about every troubling behavior pathological narcissists demonstrate: aggression when their ego is threatened, infidelity, vindictiveness, extreme envy, boasting, name-dropping, denial of any problems or wrongdoing—even workplace sabotage...When they can't let go of their need to be admired or recognized, they have to bend or invent a reality in which they remain special despite all messages to the contrary (pp. 58, 60).

Such persons who are faced with realizing they are not as special as they thought they were, experience a profound crisis of the self. They have depended on their defenses and facade precisely to keep this information at bay.

Threatened in this fashion produces an increase in paranoid thoughts (a perception that no safety exists anywhere), impaired judgement (based on artificial and inflated views of reality), volatility (which can be dangerous), as well as projection (where it is the other one who is considered to be crazy).

If these mechanisms fail, the narcissistic individual begins to lose his or her grip on reality and becomes irrational.

West (2017) called such people "Other blamers." It is important that the "other" be blamed, because such people have poor self-esteem as a result of poor shame tolerance.

West (Ibid) argued:

> As children, Other-blamers were likely exposed to developmental or attachment trauma, such as abusive, shaming, rejecting, or neglectful parenting…These experiences can cause children to feel unloved, unprotected, and inadequate (p. 247).

The other-blaming attitude is fueled by a deep personal fear of being found unworthy. West (Ibid) pointed out that domestic abuse and violence typically occurs when "the abuser feels challenged, demeaned, or rejected by a partner (Ibid, p. 248)."

Social groups can come to oppose each other in this way. Hitler, for example, admired the American racial issue and imported elements of it in his persecution of the Jews (See Ross). Disparities between levels of education may collide. It is estimated, for example, that in America about half the population never reads or rarely reads books. Further the books read are rarely academic (Brown, 2017). There is also an especially rapid increase in the use of social media among people under thirty years of age where content is routinely not demanding and is of little interest to older groups (see Media).

When narcissistic and other-blaming people find themselves cornered, they commonly lash out and can be violent. This echoes their background lack of safety, comfort, or love. Cornered, their only concern is for what is perceived as survival.

Demeaning others helps to depersonalize them and make it seem their thoughts and feelings are irrelevant. Lying to others is commonplace.

Living with such a person over time is to have one's sense of reality constantly challenged and demeaned. Perceptions based on consensual reality are considered a threat by the narcissistic person. *They* are the adequate ones. *They* determine the reality in the home, relationship, or work environment. It is dangerous to associate with others outside the context as those associations, based on reality, make it more difficult to conform to the distorted reality at home.

What one loses in such a situation is his or her *voice*. No one listens. No one cares. No one wants to hear anything except the approved line. This fact itself is a fundamental element in psychological abuse.

The one with delusions of adequacy who establishes the dimensions of the relationship—deaf to input from others —creates a crippling and abusive context for everyone affected by it.

This is a problem that is created by damaged parents— which we all are to one degree or another. It is a problem that involves millions of people.

REFERENCES

Brown, B. A Snapshot of American Reading Habits in 2017 https://geediting.com/snapshot-american-reading-habits-2017/

Eliade, M.   The Sacred and the Profane: The Nature of Religion. Harcourt, 1957/1959.

Eliade, M. Myth and Reality. Harper, 1963.

Fonagy, P. Attachment Theory and Psychoanalysis. Other, 2001.

Girard, R. Violence and the Sacred. Norton, 1979.

Girard, R. The Scapegoat. Johns Hopkins, 1989.

Jung, C.G. Man and His Symbols. Dell, 1964.

Kernberg, O. F. Borderline Conditions and Pathological Narcissism. Aronson, 1975.

Kohut, H. How Does Psychoanalysis Cure? Chicago, 1984.

Media.   https://www.statista.com/statistics/274829/age-distribution-of-active-social-media-users-worldwide-by-platform/

Mika, E. Who Goes Trump? Tyranny as a Triumph of Narcissism. In The Dangerous Case of Donald Trump. B. Lee (Ed.) St. Martin's, 2017

Malkin, C. Pathological Narcissism and Politics: A Lethal Mix. In The Dangerous Case of Donald Trump. B. Lee (Ed.) St. Martin's, 2017

Rosin, H. Even Madder Men. New York Times, 11-22-13.

Ross, A. How American Racism Influenced Hitler. https://readersupportednews.org/opinion2/277-75/49707-how-american-racism-influenced-hitler

West, H. In Relationship with an Abusive Parent. In The Dangerous Case of Donald Trump. B. Lee (Ed.) St. Martin's, 2017.

Wittgenstein, L. Philosophical Investigations. Macmillan, 1953.

ATONEMENT

It is the afternoon of the first day of the new year. I have been thinking about my parents and my long struggles with them. The time has come when, after almost four score years, I have finally matured out of my early self-centered blaming of them. This has allowed me to have a different view.

Many of us have been left to struggle with conflicting feelings about parents whose performance was compromised enough to cause an estrangement. Since this was true of me, it has been a significant interest in my learning, my psychotherapy, and in my attempts to grow.

The issue is simple to state: a child cannot bring to his or her parents the healing they cannot bring to the child.

Of course, all of us are compromised in several different ways, and all of us are approximate parents. Winnicott (1992) talked about a "good enough mother." This is a happy phrase that can be used to speak about a mother who does enough things right that she does not do great damage to the parent-child relationship.

There are many ways in which such a relationship can go wrong. Also, nature in its very structure is perhaps unfair to mothers as it loads them with the primary responsibility of caring for an infant. And, of course, mothers have had a childhood of their own—with parents who were adequate or not in some fashion—so they have childhood issues of their own to work through.

We still live in a time when people do not as a rule routinely seek psychotherapy of any significant depth. As Americans, we are still not eager to enter psychotherapy except when we have some significant issue we can't overcome, or we have some kind of specific problem. For this reason, American psychotherapy has tended to be problem focused instead of exploratory. It has also tended to be of shorter duration.

American psychotherapy is routinely practiced on the level of the patient's (client's) conscious constructions. At times there is a dialog between the therapist and the client about what the therapy will be about, how long it will take, and the exact method to be used. All of this is done in order to give the client a "say" in the treatment.

The upshot of this kind of attitude is that parents are not likely to seek psychotherapy for themselves unless there is stress in the marital relationship or the parent-child interaction is problematic. Therapy is conducted until the problem is tolerably resolved and then suspended.

Much of the support for this problem-centered approach is laid at the door of American WASP attitudes about "pulling yourself up by the bootstraps," "being self-sufficient," "not crying over spilled milk," or some similar principle designed to urge toughening up.

The wide spread employment of problem-solving therapy can result in an unfortunate shortcoming. This involves the common practice of people, other than possibly Jewish people, of not thinking of psychotherapy as beneficial to the development of their own lives. Thus, we are sold on education for the most part. We are sold on the benefits of world travel. We are even (somewhat) sold on regular medical and dental care.

Exploring what we don't know about our own minds, however, remains over the line.

Besides protracted psychotherapy is a significant investment, and we would rather have a new car—like everyone else has.

This set of values isn't restricted to those in the business community, though it figures heavily there. Where one's worth is measured in terms of the things one has, ideas and awareness tend to take second place.

Because of these such issues, significant psychotherapy, like advanced study, tends to only be sought by a certain group.

The pathology of my childhood home was the result of a very bright, narcissistic mother and a very bright, overly passive father. I have written extensively about these people before (Gill, 2015, 2015b).   Newer information I have learned follows. I intend to use this as an example.

Prior to my birth, I had an older brother who died as a baby. This was a topic that was absolutely out of bounds in my childhood home. Whatever was spoken about this child was kept from me.   Even the place where he was buried was not revealed, though my parents visited it in secret by themselves.   It is likely I was thought of as a miraculous replacement.

My mother's father was a harsh and autocratic man who at one point was the marshal of the town in which we lived. My grandmother was complicit with him. The family could be described as fundamentalist. There were eight children, of whom my mother was by far the brightest. She was a talented actress who was able to excel in school and who studied for her master's degree.

She married late to my father who was an electrical engineer and who studied advanced mathematics.   My mother was the "strong" one in the relationship. Both of my parents were in their mid-thirties when they wed.

I was born into a family grieving for the loss of a child by a father who was doing all he could to be pleasing and to survive—and a mother who was riddled with grief and with a new baby on her hands. All of this went well until it was time for individuation.

My becoming a separate person was more than my mother could manage. I had been her comfort, and she had used me for that purpose. It was mostly about her. As I separated from her, however, I was found to think about myself instead of her—and to think differently and apart from her.

My mother's grief became her rage. This was rage against me for spoiling her dream; rage against life for the cruel turn it had sent her way; rage against all the pain and struggles of her background; and perhaps even rage at her existential situation.

My mother tried her best to get me to give up myself and become who she wanted me to be. I don't know how I sensed this, but somehow, I knew that my mother was trying to steal my soul. I was terrified of her. I also dimly understood that if she found out where I was, it would be curtains for me (for my own integrity).

I did everything I could to avoid her. If required to comply, I complied on the surface as far as I felt I could and still retain myself. Throughout this time, she made it clear I was "the problem." I was a "bad kid." She became psychologically and physically abusive of me. She would go into rages that were terrifying.

I believe my earliest internalizations were of the self my mother needed me to be instead of the self I was. Then, after I separated from her in the family constellation, I became the problem. When my brother was born, he became the "good kid."

My models during this time were 1) manipulative competition (mother), 2) passive agreement (father), or (3) the authoritarian culture in which we lived. Manipulative competition won. I entered into a highly risky war with my mother even though such an endeavor was very much beyond me.

The result of this sort of development was the notion I was unacceptable, which had been drilled into my head by my mother and father juxtaposed with the success I had in thwarting my mother's desires. Thus, I was both good and bad.

Neither of my parents were easy to push over. My mother, especially, demanded to be in charge. My father supported this, at least on the surface. My mother had to win, a trait I rarely saw her give up.

It was this need to be in charge that ruined our interaction and made it impossible for us to have any sort of healthy relationship. Resonant joining was simply beyond her, at least as far as I was concerned. She did some of this with my brother.

I was too young to know much about psychoanalysis and so it didn't occur to me that my mother was likely treating me in the fashion she had been treated by her authoritarian and cold parents. Obedience had been demanded, and it was simply assumed this was the proper way to conduct a family.

I internalized this parent who was short on loving kindness and vulnerable softness and who was long on rules and punishment.

This stance of hers likely had to do with a longing for control after she had been hurt by so many things she could not control. Fate had dealt her brutal blows: abuse, cultural status as a second-class gender, the death of an infant, and now a child who would not comply. I think as her grief transformed into rage, she was determined to seize control of me or die trying. It was certainly a pitched battle.

My father was afraid of her. Being the youngest in his family and used to being bossed around by sisters (as well as adored by them), he made his way by pleasing and making no waves. My mother was likely more of a handful than he had counted on as her wrath was formidable.

I was a child and could see none of this. I only saw a frightening mother and a largely absent father. I felt alone in this family that never ceased to remind me throughout my growing years how defective I was.

So, I hated them with that twisted logic that only hates what it wants to love.

Transcending this matrix was a major project and was not easy. I largely lived away from them, though I needed their financial support while I was in school. I also subsequently spent about seventeen years in psychoanalytic psychotherapy. The results of that were: I found the negative view I had of myself was not real, my parents were compromised, I was not the narcissistic disaster area I thought I was, and, as a child, I didn't have a chance.

This was nothing short of a transformation to a whole new life. It will always be amazing to me the power of significant psychotherapy. We all know a disease will kill us. But we don't often think that a word will as well. Moving from the context of one's identity to a territory outside of that context is an amazing, shattering, and ultimately profound event.

But now I realize I have always been harsh toward my parents. True, they did what they did. True, I was the one who had the dent, and it was up to me to fix it. True, anger was appropriate. But anger isn't all there was, and I am a healer after all.

I have often imagined a situation in which people logically similar to my parents came to see me for psychotherapy. What would that be like? This kind of thinking enabled me to shift from the perspective of a child to the perspective of an adult: a peer. Could I help them?

It is an odd thought. Neither of my parents would ever consider psychotherapy. They would also be difficult to treat.

My father would be the easiest. I have worked with patients who have been squashed by the women in their backgrounds. These people have survived by attempting to please those with whom they dealt. It is their main strategy. Hidden behind such a strategy is a frightened self that dares not be authentic, because it is too risky. It becomes a life of survival, not a life of living. Minus the more manipulative elements, it is Willy Loman.

If he would "take hold" of such treatment, my father could make progress. It would be slow and tedious, but he would need to experience an interpersonal reality different from the one he knew and relied upon. This would be the case as his pattern of living was originally developed, because it seemed to be a safe place. The hardest thing to challenge is one's safety system.

But with enough empathic support, he could have done it. And once he allowed himself to see life could be different —could really be different—he would likely continue to heal.

I'm not sure about my mother. She could be as brutal as I assume she had been treated herself. There was a sadistic element to this brutality of hers. Part of her enjoyed it. She loved a fight—and was almost always in one. I find it hard to imagine my mother trusting another with her well-being. Weakness would likely terrify her.

Like many people who have experienced trauma, my mother had a kind of attack force always at the ready. This was to be deployed in the event of anything that might be considered threatening or hurtful. When her defenses were up, and the attack force was alerted, she was formidable indeed.

My mother strongly defended her parents and talked about what fine people they were. This always reminded me of Alice Miller's (1983) comment about how she shuddered whenever she heard a patient say he or she had a perfect childhood. My mother's brutality had to come from somewhere, and I imagine it was meted out by my grandfather. He was a sour man who was impressed by his own stature.

My mother's sisters were far less bright and capable, except one: the oldest. She was a perceptive, warm, and caring person who was a life-long teacher. The others simply fit in where they could.

An early fist-pounding feminist before such people were organized, my mother at times seemed to be at war with everyone. She was disgusted by women who made themselves up and were beautiful objects. She was also disgusted by men who were boisterous and filled with hot air. She was good at her art and was proud of this. But the anger was everywhere.

A therapist would have to be able to contain this anger, as my mother would certainly be critical of the treatment. This containment would have to continue until my mother was willing to risk a look at what was beneath it: enormous pain. The pain would threaten to swamp her, and she would be terrified. Whether or not my mother would allow herself to move to this level is doubtful. She was too good at fighting.

Still, like my father—and like all of us—there was a little child inside my mother who wasn't so sure about the big world. Also, this child had been treated brutally when it was a child. It would have no reason to imagine things would be different.

My mother's esteem would require much rebuilding. Her need to prevail would be a constant trait. This would have to be played out in interactions with the therapist. Thus, the therapist would have to be fairly resolved in terms of his or her own sense of worth to keep from competing with my mother—which would be a collusion.

Whether or not psychotherapy would be able to help her would swing on how she bought into it. It would be of critical importance that she see a non-authoritarian therapist who could treat her with genuine warmth. This would help her lower her blast shields. If she could meet psychotherapy with anything other than massive resistance or dismissal, she could begin to make progress. This would be difficult as she would have to confront the edges of her awareness and her need to be in control.

I am simply not sure how far my mother could progress. She obviously had a surfeit of tragedy against which she needed to defend. I see her as a tragic figure.

My own therapist frequently commented about how important it was for me to *not* get caught in any particular point of view. Frankly I was afraid of points of view. My childhood had been one in which my parents defended their turf with all they had. They were right by their own decree. And they were right about everything.

I avoided them. But I have found I have stood in an oppositional space long enough. It is time to move to compassion. I have stuck my toe in that water before, to be sure, but gingerly. Now I see my parents operating with enormous scars in a family they did not know how to manage.

The best thing about them was their fierce devotion to education. Both my brother and I finished our Ph.Ds and became professional people.   My parents would have approved of that.

But, at this juncture, I would like to atone to their memory for the blindness and incapacity I had in dealing with them.   I could not have known otherwise at the time. But I am sensitive to their anguish, and I could not get clear enough myself during their lifetimes to help them.   The best I could do was to stay away.

I have imagined seeing them again, sitting across from them, and trying to have a conversation.   It is a hard thing to imagine.   While they were still in full command of their faculties, my mother would be highly defended, and my father would be reflexively supportive of her.

Toward the end of her life, my mother softened somewhat.   Some interaction was possible with her, but I was not yet in a place sufficiently removed in psychological space from her to be able to be unguarded myself.   My father developed a slow dementing process. Both were elderly.   My mother died at age eighty-nine, and my father died at age ninety-six.

I wish I could cast a healing veil across my parents and cure them of their pain.   I have spent my life trying to cure my own as well as that of my patients.   Curing my parents is not something I was able to do, but I want to say I finally can see them from a different vantage point than from one aggrieved.   I am glad I don't live in their context.   I would not do that.   And they would not ever live in mine.

My own son has three sons of his own. He is a bright, and kind, attorney in Washington D.C. I love to visit and play with his kids. They always beg me to stay when I leave. I hope the curse ended with me. Someone has to be the salamander who first crawls out on the sand.

So, in the end, I don't know what kind of atonement I can make to my parents. I would hope I could have real compassion for them and be gentle with them.

PART II

Each of us has to come to a reckoning with the people we have known, especially with our parents and those who have been close to us. It is an essential part of maturity.

As parents all of us make mistakes. Some of these are minor and some are not. Patenting is simply too hard a task to do effortlessly, and few of us have any reasonable sort of training for the job.

The most common training we have is the model of our own parents, the influence of our peers, or random things we have read. Of the experience itself, we know little. Our own parents were likely untrained themselves and were left to rely on what was available to them—which was likely no more than is available to us ourselves.

The chances are excellent our parents made some pretty enormous mistakes, and, once these mistakes were made, they didn't know how to compensate for them. Years went by with no resolution.

Part of understanding oneself involves understanding one's parents and one's background. One by one the wounds are examined, clarified, and made real. The wounded selves we have become slowly appear in a real sense. What are we to do with these wounds?

Among the rainbow of emotions we have experienced, we have been hurt, angry, fearful, as well as feeling lost. What have we done with these feelings? Have they been allowed? Have they been hidden?

As children we were not able to see our parents' limitations and compensate for them. We just got hurt. But now we are adults, our childhood understandings and coping patterns don't fit well with our adult contexts. Besides, dragging a big bag of wrongs around with us all the time is exhausting and limiting.

Our parents likely treated us in ways they knew. They were not allowed to learn other ways. Also, they were invested in their methods and behavior.

Campbell (1949) argued that one cannot achieve atonement with a parent until the preparatory work has been completed. This requires the journey of growing up and becoming capable in and of oneself. One must become a full person in a world of full persons in order to comprehend what that means.

This is to say that moving beyond childhood hurts and the world they represent requires one to become an adult in an adult context—to have left the childhood context behind. Only then is it possible to allow the parents to be seen in an adult context instead of the context of one's childhood.

Especially if one has been a parent, one has practiced in the parent capacity in addition to the childhood capacity. Atonement—the at-one-ment—is a state in which the now adult child says to the parents, "We are equal."

Thus, the now adult child with all of his or her strengths and weaknesses speaks to his or her parents with all their strengths and weaknesses—*equal to equal.*

Such an equality requires one to know and understand who one is and to be able to see the parents as real people with real approximate backgrounds and real parents of their own.

One was hurt by parents who were unable to do any better. One hurts one's own child in the same way. Atonement involves the realization: I too know what it is like to have an approximate history and to have been wounded by life and others—*and*—I know you have had an approximate history as well and have been wounded by life and others.

To be able to move to such a position requires a capacity for empathy. I need to be able to tolerably put myself into your shoes, with your background, your psychology, your limits, and try to imagine life from your perspective. This is a move I cannot make if rage is the central element of my approach to the matter.

This said, there are things forgiveness cannot be. I may forgive you, because I realize you could not have done differently, but this does not change the fact you actually did what you did. That is, forgiveness does not erase history. The history is still there.

What atonement *does* do is to move one out of the resentful, victim position. That is, it wasn't so much the cruel hand of fate that hurt me. It was limited parents. I can understand that limitation and thus understand the parents—and this allows me to see how I was hurt by such limitations. It does not erase the wound. It transforms the wound. Given the childhood circumstances, the wound is understandable.

If I stay out in the sun too long without adequate preparation, I will be wounded by the sun. The sun did not deliberately set out to wound me. That's just how the sun works. I may avoid the sun ever after, but I do not *blame* the sun for the wounding.

This above logic is hard or impossible to swallow in the case of severe abuse. It may be impossible to avoid thinking of oneself as a victim in that case.

The problem with thinking of oneself as a victim is that such a position 1) binds one to an anger stance and 2) prevents one from advancing to a more synoptic position. Such a position is something along the lines of: we all hurt others, and we all are hurt by others.

Still, credit where credit is due. I still remember a young woman saying to me in a steely voice: "You can't expect someone to forgive her rapist!" No, you can't. But if such a person is genuinely interested in healing, you can help her to understand the people and situation involved in the service of being able to place these things in the larger context of life.

So, why do that? Why not be mad as hell and continue to rail against a world in which such things can happen? Why not crusade for justice? Isn't that a noble calling? No more cripples!

The truth is some people will choose this route. They will campaign and try to change the world. That is a way for them to work out their rage against injustice. It would be hard for them to do otherwise.

Such a direction and project requires a lot of energy, time, and resource. It involves a heavy emotional burden. It may be life-consuming.

Not everyone desires to spend his or her life assuaging a childhood wound. Some desire to heal as best they can from the ordeal and come to a kind of peace with life and the world. This requires moving into a position of awareness and deeper understanding.

The move from the world of the wounded child to the comprehending adult allows the adult to try to develop beyond the wound. Once the dent in the fender has been faced and accepted, it is possible to seek out what can be done with it. Is it repairable? What is possible?

When one seeks to find what is possible with one's life, one shifts into a mode of trying to maximize what is possible with what one has. This is actually a similar project to that of one who was not abused. What is possible for me?

The movement from wounded victim to resolved adult is a substantial transformation. It is a process that changes one's life. The element that works this transformation is *mercy*. This is brought about by letting go to a greater truth of reality. Instead of demanding life go my way, I allow it to go its own way.

Campbell spoke of the line from the Gospel of Matthew: "Whosoever will lose his life for my sake shall find it (16:25)." Rather than conquering life, one lets go to it.

> The meaning of this is very clear...The individual, through prolonged psychological discipline, gives up completely all attachment to his personal limitations, idiosyncrasies, hopes and fears, no longer resists the self-annihilation that is prerequisite to rebirth in the realization of truth, and so becomes ripe, at last, for the great at-one-ment (p. 237).

We may say: to tolerate reality requires us to move beyond our childhood demands and learn to be at one with who we really are and what the world really is.

Such at-one-ment with reality cannot be realized until one has adequate preparation. All profound rites require preparation. Here the preparation has to do with coming to understand why I have the thoughts and preferences I do. How have I become bound to the temptations of the Buddha: lust and fear? How can I move beyond these?

It is only when I am ready to pay the price of transformation that I can find a new life. It is only when I am ready to let the old life die that the new life can begin.

REFERENCES

Campbell, J. Transformations of Myth Through Time. Harper, 1990.

Campbell, J. The Hero with a Thousand Faces. Princeton/Bollingen, 1949/1968.

Campbell, J. The Power of Myth. Doubleday, 1988.

Eliade, M. Myth and Reality. Harper, 1963.

Eliade. M. The Sacred and the Profane: The Nature of Religion. Harcourt, 1957/1959.

Kohon, G. The Dead Mother: The Work of Andre Green. Routledge, 1999.

Gill, J.D. Circumference: A Memoir. Create Space, 2015.

Gill, J.D. The Misery of the Good Child. Create Space, 2015b.

Miller, A. The Drama of the Gifted Child: The Search for the True Self. Basic, 1997.

Winnicott, D. W. Through Pediatrics to Psycho Analysis: Collected Papers. Brunner/Mazel, 1992

HEARING AND TRAUMA

"Know Thyself" was the inscription over the front portico of the Temple of Apollo at Delphi. Such words are mighty and humbling, because, as the ancients knew, such a feat is far from easy.

They also require a mind that is curious. This in turn requires a mind that is eager to learn what it does not now understand. It requires, in short, a mind that is courageous enough to move beyond fear and hiding.

The Greeks revered such a mind. It involved being open to what it did not even realize it did not know. This, in turn, required venturing into a region of mystery—beyond the maps, the answers, one's present awareness and options.

Such a venturing is impeded by many obstacles. One can be burdened with exhausting work, the care and nourishment of children, disease, consuming requirements, and by trauma.

It is precisely the self and its ability to see itself and the world even relatively clearly that is damaged by trauma.

Furthermore, attempts to heal the effects of trauma are themselves stymied by the multiple ways in which effects of trauma wounds are layered into the very structure of the self as well as its neurophysiology.

People who see themselves as surrounded by fear and danger are different from those who see themselves surrounded by opportunities and challenges. The brains of such people are different.

Trauma is associated with this difference. Though all of us have experienced trauma in our lives to varying degrees, some trauma is more impactful. Studies in attachment theory have shown that infants who experience other than secure attachment are required to come to grips with growth interrupting experiences (Bowlby, 2005, Fonagy, 2001). When you are a child and the person upon whom you must rely for support, protection, and identity development is hurtful or negligent, you are left to cope on your own at an age too young to have the tools to accomplish that coping successfully.

The effects of this are crippling in several ways, not the least of which is that the resulting fear impedes the learning of successful coping strategies. As Freud (1989, see also Gabbard, 2000) argued, the normal growth process is overwhelmed at such points. When similar future traumas are encountered, one's coping abilities tend to *regress* back to the point of the original trauma, leaving the person overwhelmed again.

How the mother holds the child in her mind has enormous implications for how the child will be able to hold him or herself in mind—who the child will think he or she is. At a fundamental level, this requires the mother to be able to listen to the infant well enough to be able to resonate adequately with the infant's experience.

If she is not able to adequately hear the child, the mother will unwittingly create a distance between herself and the child. The resulting interaction will not be emotionally close enough for the child's optimal development. Such distance will serve as the child's sense of what "ordinary" contact is. The sharing of feelings, for example, may be off-limits.

Being heard brings about feelings of welcome and safety for the child. Conversely, not being heard leads to feelings of fear.

van der Kolk (see V, 2015) stated:

> ...attachment researchers have shown that our earliest caregivers don't only feed us, dress us, and comfort us when we are upset; they shape the way our rapidly growing brain perceives reality. Our interactions with our caregivers convey what is safe and what is dangerous: whom we can count on and who will let us down; what we need to do to get our needs met. This information is

embodied in the warp and woof of our brain circuitry and forms the template of how we think of ourselves and the world around us. These inner maps are remarkably stable across time.

Also:

Social support is not the same as merely being in the presence of others. The critical issue is reciprocity: being truly heard and seen by the people around us, feeling that we are held in someone else's mind and heart. For our physiology to calm down, heal, and grow we need a visceral feeling of safety. No doctor can write a prescription for friendship and love: These are complex and hard-earned capacities (Ibid).

What this suggests is that, at the very beginnings of their lives, infants either feel safe or unsafe. This reaction is directly a result of the experience of the environment in which they live—the context, the "world" as it were. Such an experience has structural consequences. Our childhood brains "wire" to the experiences we have of the contexts in which we exist. This results in an organization of brain structure and function.

Trauma results in a fundamental reorganization of the way mind and brain manage perceptions. It changes not only how we think and what we think about, but also our very capacity to think (Ibid)."

Specifically, our brains either become developed to deal with fearful or intriguing surroundings. That is, we tend to see ourselves and the world around us in different ways. If, for example, we are essentially treated as objects, we will learn that treating ourselves and others as objects is the way relationships and interactions are accomplished. If, on the other hand, we are treated with welcome, we tend to find welcome with others.

It is possible to be born into an essentially non-hearing family that lives in an essentially non-hearing sub-set of the culture. Such, for example, may be the case of a believer-family in an extremist cult. A child is such an environment would be expected to model his or her "reality" on the environment he or she knows. Thus, his or her sense of reality will be at odds with the larger culture.

In a sense this always happens. We are only able to know what we know. Our views of the world are routinely only as broad as were the views of our parents. If we are curious, we are always trying to learn what it is we don't yet know. In an important sense, we are always trying to transcend our childhood environments.

Not being heard, on the other hand, creates a wound of fear. Especially when we are infants, the help, comfort, and protection of our families is critical. If the family's focus is on discipline and compliance instead of hearing, the child's feelings tend to be ignored.

> Being frightened means that you live in a body that is always on guard. Angry people live in angry bodies. The bodies of child-abuse victims are tense and defensive until they find a way to relax and feel safe (Ibid).

The essential problem is that such people erect defenses to hide what they know about themselves and their own experiences. Thus, one is not allowed to know what one, in some sense, does know. One becomes a stranger to oneself. To compensate for feeling this deficiency, one develops a false self (Winnicott, 1992) that appears capable and then functions as this false self in interactions.

Persons who have experienced trauma learn to shut down areas of their brain that signal feelings of terror and helplessness. The problem is that these areas of the brain are also responsible for the sensations that form our self-awareness. Essentially, one dulls everything in order to dull the pain.

Such persons experience a hole in their sense of self. Attempts to deal with the pain of this absence include mood dysregulation, substance abuse, social disruption, and various psychological and medical problems.

Furthermore, children who have been abused or neglected routinely become difficult to manage. They are often angry, disobedient, and out of control. They become problems in school. They are routinely passed from treatment professional to treatment professional and given a long list of diagnoses—none of which are helpful. Others develop a kind of reverse condition in which the child is so overwhelmed he or she becomes significantly fearful, shy, and withdrawn.

There are several ways to help such children and adults. Part of this involves re-acquainting people with the body sensations they have muted off or the chronic tension they display around others. Another is the experience of a caring and resonant other in a context of welcome and safety.

Van der Kolk (Ibid) put it this way:

> [Consider] the many branches of the vagus nerve—Darwin's "pneumogastric nerve"—which connects numerous organs, including the brain, lungs, heart, stomach, and intestines.) The Polyvagal Theory provided us with a more sophisticated understanding of the biology of safety and danger, one based on the subtle interplay between the visceral experiences of our own bodies and the voices and faces of the people around us. It explained why a kind face, or a soothing tone of voice can dramatically alter the way

we feel. It clarified why knowing that we are seen and heard by the important people in our lives can make us feel calm and safe, and why being ignored or dismissed can precipitate rage reactions or mental collapse. It helped us understand why focused attunement with another person can shift us out of disorganized and fearful states."

In essence this suggests it is important to experience an interaction in which one may feel the elements of secure attachment and interpersonal attunement.

Such an experience helps one focus on one's own emotions and fearful tension, but also allows for a close, safe, open resonance with a non-critical other. This ability to be completely who one is with another while at the same time feeling safe is a hallmark of mental health. It is only through genuine and safe connections that we are able to live meaningful and satisfying lives.

It is not surprising that those who are afraid have trouble moving forward into that which they do not know. Such people are routinely more comfortable with what they do know as well as focusing on their own past—which is thought to be known. In short, those who are afraid want to go home in search of an experience of the understanding and comfort they thought they had.

In some forms of religion people similarly seek to attach to a comforting God figure to duplicate the experience they had with their parents—to buffer the adult experience of being alone and responsible. If their parents were resonant, warm, and welcoming, they will seek such attributes in a deity. If, on the other hand, their parents were authoritarian and judgmental, they will seek such attributes in a deity. Such adjustments tend to duplicate in adulthood the contexts and arrangements of childhood.

Religion extends significantly into the areas of race and gender. Evangelicals and fundamentalist Christians routinely favor an emphasis on the patriarchy, especially the white, straight patriarchy. For example, this extends far beyond the Mormon prophet Joseph Smith's drive into polygamy. Here women, African Americans, and gender variant people are not given equal weight with white, straight males. This in turn leads to a tendency to minimize such people or not hear their voices and concerns adequately.

One place such a process occurs is in the practice of home schooling. Home schooled children are kept from the socializing experiences of a diverse population in public schools (Vander, 2017). Home schooling also often follows ideas put forth by the Biblical Patriarchy Movement (BPM). This movement urges a view that the man is to be dominant in both the family and also in institutional settings.

It may be seen these notions replace individual, reciprocal human interactions with structures in which women, African Americans, and gender variant people are accorded lower stature, and whose voices are considered less than white, straight males—who are considered to hold "spiritual authority (see also Tarico, 2015)."

Such a view was forcefully challenged by feminism and by attempts to pass the Equal Rights Amendment (ERA). These practices were seen as a threat to fundamentalist and evangelical notions of masculine superiority and were vigorously opposed by a form of culture war (Du Mez, 2017). To evangelicals and those with similar views, challenging the white straight male patriarchal order is considered to be a significant error (Hessinger and Tobey, 2018).

A significant increase in rage reactions has been noted among white, Christian, fundamentalist males (Taub, 2018). Rage about the loss of social stature among these people is focused toward the broader culture that is seen to have passed them by—especially women, college-educated elites, LGBTQ people, and globalists.

So why don't people simply leave the area of their troubled lives and cross over to the area where such troubles occur far less frequently?

One answer is, as people, we don't know what we don't know. Even worse, we don't even know we don't know what we don't know.

A famous study by Kruger and Dunning (2011) found that the less capable people actually are, the more likely they are to overestimate their abilities.

I provide argument and evidence that the scope of people's ignorance is often invisible to them. This *meta-ignorance* (or ignorance of ignorance) arises because lack of expertise and knowledge often hides in the realm of the "unknown unknowns" or is disguised by erroneous beliefs and background knowledge that only appear to be sufficient to conclude a right answer. As empirical evidence of meta-ignorance, I describe the Dunning–Kruger effect, in which poor performers in many social and intellectual domains seem largely unaware of just how deficient their expertise is. Their deficits leave them with a double burden— not only does their incomplete and misguided knowledge lead them to make mistakes but those exact same deficits also prevent them from recognizing when they are making mistakes and other people are choosing more wisely (Dunning, 2011).

In this situation one feels one's understanding extends farther than it does. The problem is that one has not developed the kinds of knowing that would allow one to become aware of what one does not know. That is, being able to see what one does not know requires a different kind of seeing than one has now. Also, needless to say, such knowing would render one's current outlook inadequate.

One way to guard against an awareness of the possibility one's awareness might be inadequate is to suggest all knowledge is opinion. Further, all opinions might be held to be equal. Here differences may be reduced to "That's just your opinion." If all knowledge is held to be opinion, it is not necessary for one to learn any more than one already knows—one already has an opinion, and it is just as good as anyone else's.

Of course, knowledge and opinion are quite different things. They are different in precisely that knowledge can be backed up with evidence and proof, whereas opinions just need to be held (see Austin, 1961, Wittgenstein, 1953). In this way opinions are similar to beliefs.

All of us experience the Dunning-Kruger effect to some degree or another. We assume our knowledge is adequate when it is not. We may loudly reject new input, because it does not square with what we currently know. Certainly, it is easy to imagine a person who has been raised in a fearful context sees things differently from someone who has not been so raised or is so raised to a significantly lesser degree.

Some estimates suggest that upwards of forty percent of American people entertain fearful outlooks on life (See Taub, Ibid.). These people tend to be less educated, more authoritarian, more rural, more drawn to fundamentalist religion, and more cut off from mainline society than others.

Clearly this is too large a group to ignore or polarize in an us-them fashion. Treating such people with disavowal and alterity solves nothing. Engaging in a war with them is pointless, though it is common for people who are fearful to react in hostile and oppositional ways. The Dali Lama is reported to have said, "Compassion is the radicalism of our time." It is incumbent upon us to find ways to help each other.

A major problem is that few of us like to hear about what we do not know. A significant way to prevent such hearing lies in political power. Messages can be minimized, countered, or reframed by the power structure to prevent their dissemination and adoption.

Autocracy, anger, and resistance is routinely the result of hurt that was experienced at the hands of parents, teachers, and authority figures who were similarly hurt themselves. Such people may have some awareness of their hurt but lack awareness of the extent or kind of that hurt.

Sometimes one must leave one's family to find mental health and peace of mind. One may even have to leave one's social group, cultural sub-set, or environment. The context always forces an ontology (theory of what is real). It is only by finding a way to step outside such a context that one becomes able to see where one has been. It is said the fish will be the last thing to discover the water. This is true, because, try as it might, water is everywhere.

We may say the fish's brain has wired to water. To such a brain, water is normal. There is no perceived need to change. Not-water would be weird and seem wrong. Let's hear it for water!

We are the fish. We need help to find what we don't know and to accept the reality of who we and other people truly are. Each one who helps us feel safe and welcome while we explore new understandings and experience helps us and the entire culture to become more healthy and humane.

REFERENCES

Austin, J.A. Truth. In Philosophical Papers. J.O. Urmson and G.J. Warnock (Eds.). Oxford, 1961.

Bowlby, J. A Secure Base: Parent-Child Attachment and Healthy Human Development. Basic, 1988.

Dunning, D. Confident Idiots. Pacific Standard. 11, 12-14.

Du Mez, K. Donald Trump and Militant Evangelical Masculinity. Religion and Politics, 01-17-17.

Freud, S. and Strachey, J. Introductory Lectures on Psychoanalysis. Liveright, 1989.

Gabbard, G. O. Psychodynamic Psychiatry: In Clinical Practice. American Psychiatric Press, 2000.

Hessinger, R., and Tobey, K. President Trump gets a Stormy Daniels Bump with Evangelicals. Cleveland. com. 04-11-18. http://www.cleveland.com/opinion/index.ssf/2018/04/president_trumps_stormy_daniel.html

Kruger, J. and Dunning, D. Unskilled and Unaware of It: How Difficulties in Recognizing One's Own Incompetence Lead to Inflated Self Assessments. Journal of Personality and Social Psychology, 1999, Vol 77, No. 6, pp. 1121-1134.

Tarico, V.   The Perverse Obsessions of Right-Wing Patriarchal Christians. Salon, 06-13-15.

Taub, A. On Social Media's Fringes: Growing Extremism Targets Women. New York Times, 05-19-18. https://www.nytimes.com/2018/05/09/world/americas/incels-toronto-attack.html

van der Kolk, B. A.   Quotes.   https://www.goodreads.com/author/quotes/290396.Bessel_A_van_der_Kolk

van der Kolk, B. A.   The Body Keeps the Score: Brain, Mind, and Body in the Healing of Trauma.   Penguin (Reprint Edition), 2015

Vander, T. Biblical Patriarchy in Doctrine and Practice: An Analysis of Evangelical Christian Homeschooling. Intermountain West Journal of Religious Studies, Vol 8, No. 1, 2017.

Winnicott, D. W. Through Pediatrics to Psycho Analysis: Collected Papers. Brunner/Mazel, 1992.

Wittgenstein, L. Philosophical Investigations. Macmillan, 1953.

THE GNOSTIC GOSPELS AND PSYCHOANALYTIC AWARENESS

Ancient mythology and religion were an attempt to understand humankind and the world in which it found itself. Mythology, as Campbell (1949, 1985, 1987, 1988, 1990) pointed out, involved ways to account for what was real. It also tried to account for what mattered.

These bits of information from ancient times, which have to do with the themes that have supported human life, built civilizations, and informed religions over the millennia, have to do with deep inner problems, inner thresholds of passage...People say that what we're all seeking is a meaning for life. I don't think that's what we're really seeking. I think that what we're seeking is an experience of being alive, so that our life experiences on the purely physical plane will have resonances within our own innermost being and reality, so that we actually feel the rapture of being alive. That's what it's all finally about, and that's what these clues help us to find within ourselves (Campbell, 1988, pp. 4,5).

The Greeks, in addition to their mythology, also developed a coherent philosophy. Early philosophers in Greece attempted to find in the poems and early religious practices themes that could be formally stated. They also indulged in speculations about the nature of reality.

Thilly and Wood (1914/1957) stated:

The speculative impulse first finds genuine expression in the Ionian physicists, the Pythagoreans, Heraclitus, the Eleatics, Empedocles, the Atomists and Anaxagoras, who attempt to explain phenomena by natural causes and without appeal to mystical beings (p. 20).

Thales, for example, stated that all things are transformed from water (Ibid. p. 21). This is a metaphysical notion. Here matter is not created by gods or carried on the backs of fantastic creatures. However naively conceived, it is a physical process and is considered rational.

Religion was different. Even in ancient Greece it was either the anthropomorphic religion of the gods of Olympus, who displayed human emotions and a concern for the lives of people, or the mystery religions which were concerned with the dying and rising resurrection of life.

Campbell (1988) said:

> What is a god? A god is a personification of a motivating power or a value system that functions in human life and in the universe —the powers of your own body and of nature. *The myths are metaphorical of spiritual potentiality in the human being, and the same powers that animate our life animate the life of the world* [my italics] (p. 22).

> Myths are clues to the spiritual potentialities of the human life...your own meaning is that you're there...[myths] teach you that you can turn inward, and you begin to get the message of the symbols...Myth helps you to put your mind in touch with this experience of being alive. It tells you what it is (p. 6)

The Jewish religion had a different slant.

> ...the biblical tradition [however] is a socially oriented mythology. Nature is condemned...when nature is thought of as

evil, you don't put yourself in accord with it, you control it, or try to... (Ibid. pp. 23, 24).

By 3000 BCE ancient Semitic tribes had spread along important trade routes in Mesopotamia. Ur, a Mesopotamian city, "is named in the Bible as the place from which Abraham and his family set out on their travels...This departure...marks the beginning of the story of the Hebrews, or Jews (see Jews)."

In *Genesis* Abraham is the patriarch of a nomadic tribe. The story has him moving through Mesopotamia (from Ur to Harran) and then down into Canaan—a land which, God promises, his descendants will inherit.

Many tribes move with their flocks among the settled cities of Mesopotamia and Phoenicia. No doubt several, from time to time, have charismatic leaders long remembered by their descendants. There is no reason to doubt that a figure such as Abraham exists, and scholars put his likely date at about 1800 BC. What makes him significant is the idea of his pact with God, by which God will help Abraham's people in return for their fulfilling God's law. This is the covenant at the heart of the story of the Hebrews (Ibid.).

Thus, the basis of the Jewish religion is the fulfillment of God's law. It is this law that binds the Jewish people together and allows them to preserve their culture.

Differentiating between in-group and out-group status has always been important to organized groups. Campbell (1986) argued that it is of prime importance to a culture or a group to suppress "the natural impulse to mercy (p. 16)."

> So that one of the first concerns of the elders, prophets, and established priesthoods of tribal or institutionally oriented mythological systems has always been to limit and define the permitted field of expression of this expansive faculty of the heart, holding it to a fixed focus within the field exclusively of the ethnic monad, while deliberately directing outward every impulse to violence (Campbell, 1988).

Thus, it was that mythologies and religions routinely had two purposes. The first was to account for transcendent realities, and the second was to govern the daily lives of people.

It may be seen that mythology, religion, metaphysics, as well as abstract reasoning routinely swing on the use of metaphor. Thus, Thales knew very well everything was not composed of liquid. His notion was that things transformed from water—and therefore could be said to be water "in essence."

Metaphors seek to create a direct emotional experience or connection rather than to simply describe something. For this reason, they are ideally suited to the feeling life.

Campbell also argued:

> The life of a mythology derives from the vitality of its symbols as metaphors delivering, not simply the idea, but a sense of actual participation in such a realization of transcendence, infinity, and abundance... Indeed the first and most essential servicer of a mythology is this one, of opening the mind and heart to the utter wonder of all being. And the second service, then, is cosmological: of representing the universe and whole spectacle of nature, both as known to the mind and as beheld by the eye, as an epiphany of such kind that when lightning flashes, or a setting sun ignites the sky, or a deer is seen standing alerted, the exclamation "Ah!" may be uttered as a recognition of divinity (Ibid, p. 18).

Such an account points to the notion that the worlds and gods of mythology "are reference and symbolic entities which are neither places nor individuals but states of being realizable within you (p. 20)."

A mythology is, in this sense, an organization of metaphorical figures connotative of states of mind (Ibid., p. 21).

Platonic philosophy of the fifth century BCE (see Thilly and Wood, 1914/1957) made a distinction between necessary (higher) and contingent (lower) propositions. Here the contingent propositions deal with physical matters. The necessary propositions deal with eternal forms which, Plato held, lie behind the physical forms and inform them.

An example is beauty. Beauty is an eternal form. There is a concept of beauty in every culture. But exactly what each culture holds as beautiful differs. The local views of beauty get their meaning from their participation in the eternal forms. That is, the "essence" of the lower forms is the higher forms (for a critique of this position see Wittgenstein, 1953).

It is a typical claim of ancient religions, especially Greek religions, to hold that true reality lies behind and beyond the reality we experience. Plato's philosophy systematized this view.

Similar views can be found in *mystical* Judaism which was influenced by Greek thought (see Philologos).

In truth, however, the matter is thus: The upper world and the lower are established upon one and the same principle; in the lower world is Israel, in the upper world are the angels. When the angels wish to descend to the lower world, they have to don earthly garments. If this be true of the angels, how much more so of the Torah, for whose sake, indeed, the world and the angels were alike created and exist. The world could simply not have endured to look upon it. Now the narratives of the Torah are its garments. He who thinks that these garments are the Torah itself [i.e., literal interpretation] deserves to perish and have no share in the world to come. Woe unto the fools who look no further when they see an elegant robe! More valuable than the garment is the body which carries it, and more valuable even than that is the soul which animates the body. Fools see only the garment of the Torah, the more intelligent see the body, the wise see the soul, its proper being; and in the Messianic time the 'upper soul' of the Torah will stand revealed (see Zohar)."

There is considerable influence of neoplatonic ideas in the Zohar (Canney, 1976).

In similar fashion Eliade (1957) pointed out that it was a common distinction in ancient religions to hold there is a difference between the sacred and the profane. Here the profane concerns the things of the earth. The sacred concerns things of the spirit. Profane things are transitory; sacred things are static (eternal).

The concept can be illustrated by considering the notion of "time." Profane time is linear. It begins at one point and goes forward. It does not retrace itself. Sacred time, on the other hand, is static. Whenever you enter it, it is available in its fullness. The German poet Gerhart Hauptmann echoed this idea when he wrote: "Alles vergangliche ist nur ein Gleichness [everything that passes is but a reflection] (see Campbell, 1990)."

Eliade said: "The sacred always manifests itself as a reality of a wholly different order from "natural" realities (Ibid. p 10)."

> Man becomes aware of the sacred because it manifests itself, shows itself, as something wholly different from the profane. To designate the *act of manifestation* of the sacred, we have proposed the term *hierophany*...From the most elementary hierophany—e.g., manifestation of the sacred in some ordinary object, a stone or a tree—to the supreme hierophant (which, for a [orthodox] Christian, is the incarnation of God in Jesus Christ) there is no solution of continuity. In each case we are confronted by the same mysterious act...The sacred tree, the sacred stone are not adored as stone or tree; they are worshipped precisely because

they are *hierophanies*, because they show something that is no longer stone or tree but the sacred, the *ganz andere* [entirely other] (Ibid, pp 11-12.)

Rudolph Otto (1917/2012) had differentiated the *experience* of the sacred from its ethical and rational elements. The sacred, he wrote, has a *numinous* element. This numinous element "presents itself as *ganz andere*, wholly other, a condition absolutely *sui generis* and incomparable whereby the human being finds himself utterly abashed." This is the *mysterium tremendum* which is at once terrifying and fascinating.

In the ancient world one sought to live in this sacred space or as close as possible to sacred objects. For such a person acts such as eating, sex, &c. were not merely physiological. They were a sacrament, a communion with the sacred.

Eliade wrote:

When the sacred manifests itself in any hierophany, there is not only a break in the homogeneity of space; there is also revelation of an absolute reality, opposed to the non-reality of the vast surrounding expanse. The manifestation of the sacred ontologically founds the world (Ibid. p. 21)

This notion of the sacred, as being apart from the profane, was changed by Christian thinkers.

> Christianity radically changed the experience and the concept of liturgical time, and this is due to the fact that Christianity affirms the historicity of the person of Christ. The Christian liturgy unfolds in *a historical time sanctified by the incarnation of the Son of God.* The sacred time [on the other hand] periodically reactualizes in pre-Christian religions (especially in archaic religions) as *mythical time*, that is, a primordial time, not to be found in the historical past, an original time, in the sense that it came into existence all at once, that it was not preceded by another time, because no time could exist *before the appearance of the reality narrated in the myth* (Ibid. p.72).

In this sense it may be seen that orthodox Christians largely conceived of religion in terms of the profane. Thus, they emphasized their beginnings, texts, and history. The only place they could find for eternal life was at the end of this one.

Gnostic Christians, on the other hand, held that all clarity was available upon becoming enlightened. One could enter eternal life at any time, anywhere. Thus, the gnostic Christians were more influenced by Greek culture whereas the developing orthodox Christians were more influenced by the Jewish rabbinical tradition.

Gnostic writers specifically challenged the orthodox view that the person of Jesus was the Christ and that the revelation of God was contained in his (historical) events (Pagels, 1989, p. 12). To hold such a view, Heraclion claimed, was to fail to distinguish between literal and symbolic truth (Ibid). The gnostic writers held there was a profound difference between material (psychic) data on the one hand and spiritual (pneumatic) truth on the other.

Gnostic writers held that orthodox interpretations of the Biblical stories were literalistic. The gnostics held, on the other hand, these stories were actually allegorical. Gnostic interpretation allowed the true (pneumatic) meaning to be uncovered from the literal (psychic) texts. This process opened the texts to an understanding of the mysteries of existence. Such mysteries, held the Gnostics, pertain to the primal Anthropos which is the archetype of humanity. Experience of these mysteries can be found in sacred rites of many ancient people (Campbell, 1988).

To the orthodox (psychics) the gospel texts were factually true. To the pneumatics these texts were allegories or metaphors that needed to be decoded to reveal the higher meaning.

William Blake (1790-1793, see Abrams, et al, 1962) echoed this when he said:

A fool sees not the same tree that a wise man sees.

Such a sentiment is echoed in Corinthians, 2: 14-16:

For the psychic does not receive the things of the spirit of God: they are foolishness to him...

In light of this difference and during the first two centuries of the common era, debate raged over the proper way to find truth. On the one hand it was argued that truth was to be found in the correct (apostolic) texts given the correct interpretation. On the other hand, truth was to be found by a profound inner realization (Hatch, 1957).

If one were searching for an answer to the troubles of life, these are different avenues one might explore. One might, for example, seek to follow established truths and live by them. On the other hand, one might seek insight through meditation or contemplation. Such debates have had lasting impact on the ways people seek answers.

Scholars hold that the Gospel of Mark was written around the year 70 CE. The Gospels of Matthew and Luke were written, independent of each other, around the year 90 CE. The Gospel of John was written later around 100 CE (see Crossroads). These books were not written in the beginning of the Christian development and none are considered to be historically accurate. Further, there are considerable differences between them. The process of joining the Gospels of Matthew, Mark, Luke, and John along with the letters of Paul into the collection called the New Testament took place gradually over approximately 200 years from 160 to 360 CE (Pagels, 2003, p. 38).

Opinion differs as to the date of the writing of the gnostic Gospel of Thomas with some suggesting the date between 50 and 100 CE and others favoring a date late in the second century CE.

Eager to establish a stable structure for the Christian church, several writers sought to codify one set of texts which were to be considered orthodox. Similarly, other texts were considered heretical. Thus it was held by those seeking to establish an orthodoxy that only by following closely the orthodox texts could one find the answers to the dilemmas of life.

Hatch (1957) pointed out: The Greek words for belief or faith as used in the Old Testament imply a sense of trust (p. 310). This gradually came to mean "the assent to certain propositions about God (p. 311). Belief in this sense is not a vague and mystical sentiment, the hazy state of mind which precedes knowledge, but the highest form of conviction. It transcends reason in certainty (p. 312). Such a development led to the apostolic creed and to the Canon of the New Testament.

To the orthodox what separated Christianity from philosophy was "the belief that the nature of God had been made certain by revelation (which was held to be of greater veracity than reason) Ibid, p. 314)."

But once this view was held it was thought necessary to limit acceptable revelations from the many different accounts that were circulating during these first two centuries CE.

The orthodox church accepted as a standard the apostolic creed.

Hatch added:

> With this development the philosophical
> ideal of the search for truth was supplanted
> by tradition and authority (Ibid, p. 322).

It became important to have the right belief. Personal interpretation was denounced.

> Meetings of bishops were held, and *through political rather than religious means* decisions were made. These decisions, moreover, were held to be final. The acceptance of these views became as important as the belief in God and in Jesus Christ. *Approved views equalled truth* [my italics] (Ibid. pp. 327, 328).

This was a practice that had been more or less employed in the Jewish apostolic tradition. By following the correct teachings one could find favor. Thus the answers were to be found in the field of time by learning and following the approved codes.

The thinkers who were influenced by Greek ideas, however, saw things differently. The Greeks (as had the Jewish mystics) had long held that the material, known reality was only part of the whole picture.

This was to make a distinction between what was external, verifiable, and passing on the one hand and what was internal, constant, and ultimate on the other. The search in the external realm was for proof, whereas the search in the internal realm was for enlightenment.

Pagels (2003) outlined the nature of the conflict in the second century CE between the Gospel of John from the New Testament and the Gospel of Thomas from the Nag Hammadi Codex.

> While Mark, Matthew, and Luke identify Jesus as God's human agent, John and Thomas characterize him instead as God's own light in human form.

> Yet, despite these similarities, the authors of John and Thomas take Jesus' private teaching in sharply different directions. For John, identifying Jesus with the light that came into being "in the beginning" is what makes him unique—God's "only begotten son." John calls him the "light of all

humanity," and believes that Jesus alone brings divine light to a world otherwise sunk into darkness. John says that we can experience God only through the divine light embodied in Jesus. But certain passages in Thomas's gospel draw a quite different conclusion: that the divine light Jesus embodied is shared by humanity, since we are all made "in the image of God." Thus Thomas expresses what would become a central theme of Jewish—and later Christian—mysticism a thousand years later: that the "image of God" is hidden within everyone, although most people remain unaware of its presence (pp. 40-41).

Thomas thus rebukes those who seek to find Jesus or the truth by following external authority.

"There is light within a person of light, and it lights up the whole universe. If it does not shine, there is darkness." In other words, one either discovers the light within that illuminates "the whole universe" or lives in darkness, within and without (Ibid. p. 56).

The Gospel of Thomas states:

Jesus said, "If those who lead you say to you, 'See, the kingdom is in the sky,' then the birds of the sky will precede you. If they say to you, 'It is in the sea,' then the fish will precede you. Rather, the kingdom is inside of you, and it is outside of you. When you come to know yourselves, then you will become known, and you will realize that it is you who are the sons [and daughters] of the living father. But if you will not know yourselves, you dwell in poverty and it is you who are that poverty (Lambdin Translation)."

This passage could almost serve as the statement of the nature of psychoanalysis. It is absolutely imperative to come to know the self—both what it is and what it is not. This requires abilities beyond concrete (psychic) thinking.

The developmental psychologist Piaget (see Ginsberg and Opper, 1969) demonstrated that abstract thinking represented a higher level of development than concrete thinking. Importantly, abstract ability extends the field of thought to analogies and higher order relationships including nuance, and metaphor. The history of philosophical thinking functions in terms of these abilities.

Plato's philosophy required being able to think beyond concrete instances or "particulars." Wittgenstein's thinking focused on "grammar" in terms of which the use of language makes sense. Pagels (1979) in her study of developments during the time of the establishment of

Christianity similarly pointed to the difference between concrete and abstract concepts.

In Pagel's account of the first and second centuries CE it can be seen many divergent gospel accounts and texts were written. Orthodox texts alone were officially preserved. The manuscripts discovered in 1945 at Nag Hammadi in northern Egypt, for example, were excluded from orthodox canon. Because of this exclusion the texts fell into obscurity and were hidden until an earthen jar containing the manuscripts was found behind a monastery in Egypt.

Written in Coptic from the period approximately 120-150 CE, these texts, though referring to events similar to those detailed in the synoptic gospels (Matthew, Mark, Luke, and John), struck a strikingly different tone. The Gnostic texts were declared heretical by orthodox Christians in the middle of the second century CE. Pagels points out, however, the gnostics did not consider themselves to be heretics.

"Gnosos" is a Greek term that roughly means knowledge/ awareness as in knowledge/awareness of oneself or "She really *knows* me (i.e., inside-out)." To the Greeks this kind of knowing was thought different from rational knowledge. It is based on direct personal experience.

The opposite of gnostic is agnostic.

The primary enterprise of the Gnostics was to gain knowledge of the self as opposed to obedience to a slate of formal prescriptions and principles.

An example is the following from the Gospel of Thomas:

> Jesus said, "If you bring forth what is within you, what you bring forth will save you. If you do not bring forth what is within you, what you do not bring forth will destroy you (see T).

In this view, "...to know oneself, at the deepest level, is simultaneously to know God; this is the secret of *gnosis* (Ibid, xix).

That is, the deep truth of the self is a reflection of the nature of God and the great meaning. God and the true self form an entity.

In the orthodox Jewish and Christian tradition, on the other hand, God is considered other than human. Here it is held that "...a chasm separates humanity from its creator: it is God who is wholly other (Ibid)."

The Gnostic Jesus, who speaks of illusion and enlightenment instead of sin and repentance as do the orthodox, directly addresses the spiritual nature of the self. Thus when the gnostic disciple becomes enlightened, "Jesus no longer serves as his "spiritual master: the two have become equal—even identical (Pagels, 1979, p. xx)."

Orthodox Christians early set about systematizing and codifying the rituals of the faith. The nature of this process was more apparent to scholars after the discovery of the

Gnostic Gospels. Early Christianity was highly diverse during these first two hundred years of its history. Texts suggesting multiple points of view were common.

> ...by A.D. 200, the situation had changed. Christianity had become an institution headed by a three rank hierarchy of bishops, priests, and deacons, who understood themselves to be the guardians of the only "true faith." The majority of churches, among which the church of Rome took a leading role, rejected all other viewpoints as heresy (Ibid, p. xxiii).

What is currently known as Christianity was distilled from a number of different sources. It is also true that the orthodox Christians, then as now, vigorously sought to discredit and abolish sources with which they did not agree. Pagels' view is that the Gnostic texts posed "political and social implications" (i.e., threats) for the development of Christianity as an institutional religion.

> In simplest terms, ideas which bear implications contrary to that development [orthodoxy] come to be labeled as "heresy"; ideas which implicitly support it become "orthodox" (Ibid, p. xxxix).

The implication of this position is that there were organizational and exclusionary criteria employed to select texts that would further the goals of the orthodox point of view as opposed to texts that (merely) contained "spiritual" or profound insights or inspiration.

In our time the issue of indwelling factors figure in terms of psychoanalytic concepts and practice. `Here the importance of dreams, unconscious dimensions, and coming to know one's self are central as they were to the gnostics.

The notion of the "place beyond" may be seen in the mystery rites held at Eleusis (see Kerenye, 1967, Gill, 2016). These were the rites associated with the goddess Demeter and her daughter Persephone. Demeter was seen as the bestower of life: this consisted of grain for food on the lower plane and enlightenment on the higher plane.

Campbell (1990) said:

> It's my belief that St. Paul's great insight on the road to Damascus was that the death of Jesus Christ on the cross could be interpreted in terms of the mystery religions' understanding of the death and resurrection of the savior—that is, as the death of one's purely animal existence and the birth, then, of the spiritual life (p. 190).

Thus at Eleusis as at other ancient rites there was a worship of the birth and death sequences that constitute nature. It is this process that was considered sacred.

Campbell also said:

> [In the rites associated with food plants as those at Eleusis] The meditation is that we are eating divine substance and this divine substance is what is feeding us. It isn't just physical substance, and that's part of the meditation: how our whole life is supported by the giving and yielding of some transcendent power (Ibid, p. 194).

Plato's depiction of the cave metaphor in The Republic (see Plato) suggests the cave dwellers are unable to emerge into the light (i.e., gnosos) and thus transform their lives.

Simply put the orthodox followed the rules; the gnostics sought enlightenment. The orthodox movement, thus, was largely external. One *professed* certain beliefs. It was not necessary to actually *have* them. This was a system that could be monitored for compliance—as indeed it has been, often with severity, throughout its history.

The following passage from the Gospel of St. Matthew, however, came close to gnostic teaching.

"And when you pray, do not be like the show-offs! They love to stand up and pray in the synagogues and on the street corners so that everybody will see them. Remember this! They have already been paid in full. But when you pray, go to your room and close the door, and pray to your Father, who is unseen. And your Father, who sees what you do in private, will reward you (see News, p. 12).

The gnostics sought to experience directly the true self without the blindness that routinely accompanies and distorts it—much in the same way that psychoanalysis works to free individual truths from the defenses and training that keep them from realization.

Pagels (1979) outlined the nature of the conflict that arose about the nature of the resurrection. Basically the orthodox view was that the *physical* body of Christ ascended to heaven (a profane account).

What is raised is "this flesh, suffused with blood, built up with bones, interwoven with nerves, entwined with veins (a flesh) which…was born, and…dies, undoubtedly human (Ibid, p. 5).

Tertullian (see Ibid) declared "anyone who denies the resurrection *of the flesh* is a heretic, not a Christian." This, he also claimed, must be believed "because it is absurd."

The gnostic view, on the other hand, echoed earlier writings of Socrates and widely held Greek ideas that held the soul was spiritual (i.e., sacred). To these thinkers the resurrection was a spiritual vision (event).

The notion that the resurrection was a physical (empirical) act that was witnessed by only a preferred few had clear political and organizational impact. It legitimized the *authority* of those who could claim to be true successors of the apostle Peter (Ibid, p. 7). The orthodox church was built on this claim to authority.

Campbell (1986) essentially sided with the Gnostics when he wrote that to claim Jesus ascended physically to heaven is to imply that Jesus—traveling at the speed of light—has not yet cleared our galaxy. The gnostics held, rather, that Jesus moved from the denotation of the metaphor to the connotation.

> ...where those bodies went was not into outer space, but into inner space [i.e., metaphorical space]. That is to say, what is connoted by such metaphorical voyages is the possibility of a return of the mind in spirit, while still incarnate, to full knowledge of that transcendent source out of which the mystery of a given life arises into this field of time and back into which it

in time dissolves...The imagery is necessarily physical and thus apparently of outer space. The inherent connotation is always, however, psychological and metaphysical, which is to say, of inner space. When read as denoting merely specified events, therefore, the mirrored inward images lose their inherent spiritual force and, becoming overloaded with sentiment, only bind the will the more to temporality (Ibid, p.31)

The gnostic view enabled anyone whomsoever to experience transcendence at any time. All persons were eligible: rich, poor, male, female, upstanding, criminal, sick, well—all people. No authority was required, only gnostic teaching about the concepts. Clearly this would not be an easy position to police for authoritarian purity.

The orthodox held, on the other hand:

...shortly after Jesus' death, Peter took charge of the group as its leader and spokesman. According to John, he had received his authority from the only source the group recognized—from Jesus himself, now speaking from beyond the grave (Ibid, p. 9).

The gnostic view is more Buddhist-like in nature. That is to be alive in an unenlightened state is a state of spiritual death. To be awakened from this state is to be allowed to see things as they actually are.

> Jesus said: I stood in the midst of the world, and I appeared to them in flesh. I found them all drunk, I found none among them thirsting; and my soul was afflicted for the sons of men, for they are blind in their heart and they do not see. For empty they came into the world, seeking also to depart empty from the world. But now they are drunk (see T).

Thus in both Gnosticism as in psychoanalysis "drunk" is used as a metaphor to refer to distorted awareness—awareness that, further, is in need of clarification so that a meaningful life may be possible.

The point is that inner awakening is *achieved*; it is not granted as the result of obedience to a program. This is the same situation that obtains in the case of psychoanalytic awareness. The therapist helps one discover his or her self beyond the defenses and distortions that have been built up in the person's attempts to survive. This is a different undertaking and a different self for each person. It is not the result of an application of a program.

Ogden (1989) said:

As analysts, we attempt to assist the analysand in his efforts at freeing himself from forms of organized experience (his conscious and unconscious "knowledge" of himself) that entrap him and prevent him from tolerating the experience of not knowing long enough to create understandings in a different way. The value of developing new ways of knowing lies not simply in the greater self-understandings one might achieve, but as importantly in the possibility that a wider range of thoughts, feelings, and sensations might be brought into being (p. 1).

To be able to discover this kind of awareness, one must be able to see there may be a difference between how one sees things and how those things actually are. This distinction is similar to the postmodern distinction between the "given" and the "made." Here, the given is what is there. I am writing this essay on a computer. That is the given. The made is what I make out of it—the significance it may have for me.

Such a shift in awareness, however, is far from easy.

It is a terrifying experience to have your consciousness transformed (Campbell and Moyers, 1988, p. 14).

Also, in order to profitably explore the self, one needs to be able to understand metaphor and metaphorical uses of language. Here it is metaphor that opens the world beyond description.

Eliade (1957) said:

> ...symbolism [metaphor] plays a decisive part in the religious life of humanity; it is through symbols that the world becomes transparent, is able to show the transcendent (p. 130).

The gnostics followed Greek ideas in holding men and women to be equal participants. The influx of Jewish ideas into developing Christian orthodoxy made this unacceptable. It may be seen that by about the year 200 CE all the gnostic texts had been omitted from the official cannon (Pagels, 1979, p. 68). It is with this development that the feminine influence left the orthodoxy.

Pagels argued:

> Orthodox writers described the church in concrete terms because they accept the status quo; that is, they affirmed that the actual community of those gathered for worship *was* the church. Gnostic Christians dissented. Confronted with those in the churches whom they considered ignorant, arrogant, or self-interested, they refused to

agree that the whole community of believers, without further qualification, constituted "the church." Dividing from the majority over such issues as the value of martyrdom, they intended to discriminate between the mass of believers and those who truly had gnosis, between what they called the imitation, or the counterfeit, and the true church (Ibid. p. 129).

Gnostic writers criticized the orthodox by pointing out that all members did not live in holiness or really keep the commandments.

The gnostic understands Christ's message not as offering a set of answers, but as encouragement to engage in a process of searching (Ibid, p 135).

Clearly speaking of orthodox practices, Camus (1956) called modern Christianity a giant laundering venture that has run out of soap. The point is that one goes through the rituals and motions, but the effective agent is now missing —the "profound experience—die ganz Andere."

In the words of a Valentinian writer, since human beings created the whole language of religious expression, so, in effect, humanity created the divine world: "...and this [Anthropos] is really he who is God over all Pagels, p. 148)."

This is an amazingly similar idea to those of Wittgenstein (1953), namely, that it is the grammar of the language that allows for understanding.

Anthropos, above, is humanity.

Again, such a view may be found in Jewish mysticism:

> The universe began not with an atom or a subatomic particle, but with the thought of creation which encompassed a world in which every human being would enjoy total happiness and fulfillment, free from any form of chaos or pain (see Kabbalah).

For gnostics, exploring the psyche became explicitly what it is for many people today implicitly—a religious quest (Ibid.).

In the gnostic view, again, it is not sin that results in human suffering, but ignorance. The notion was that most people live in a kind of oblivion or unconscious state. They are drunk. Further this self ignorance is a type of self destruction.

Pagels wrote:

> ...gnosticism shares with psychotherapy a fascination with the nonliteral significance

of language, as both attempt to understand the internal quality of experience. The psychoanalyst C.G. Jung has interpreted Valentinus' creation myth as a description of the psychological processes. Valentinus tells how all things originate from "the depth," the "abyss"—in psychoanalytic terms, from the unconscious. From that "depth" emerge Mind and Truth, and from them, in turn, the Word (Logos) and Life. And it was the word that brought humanity into being. Jung read this as a mythical account of the origin of human consciousness (Pagels, p. 160).

A parallel account of things originating from the "depth" and the "abyss" may be found in the writings ascribed to Hermes Trismegistus (H) from roughly the same period as the gnostic gospels.

It is not surprising that ancient notions of enlightenment influenced Freud who was conversant with Hassidic mysticism.

Of Freud, Roith (1987) stated:

...his first experience was that of a son a Jewish parents, both of whom were born in the proverbial ghetto or hamlet of Eastern Europe where Jews had lived, in the main in isolated communities and in a state of

strict religious orthodoxy for hundreds of
years (p. 2).

Both Freud's mother and caretaker, whom he adored,
were devout. It is also the case that Hassidim was a
movement that began in the eighteenth century in Eastern
Europe where Freud was born. Freud's father, grandfather,
and his great grandfather were all hassids.

Berke (2015, see Karnacology) stated that Freud tended
to play down his religious orientation in his professional
life.

> However, more recent studies, especially
> those of David Bakan, Yosef Yerushalmi,
> Marianne Krüll, Emanuel Rice, and Tom
> Keve show a very different and more
> complicated Freud. This Freud emerged
> from a deeply religious Hassidic
> background, with generations of
> distinguished rabbis and scholars on both
> his maternal, paternal and marital sides.
> They show that Freud was very
> knowledgeable about Jewish ideas and
> practices and that he was conversant with
> both Hebrew and Yiddish.

Berke argued that "Freud wavered between his identity as
a rational scientist and his explorations of subjective

worlds…(p. 1). He also argued that psychoanalysis opened the door to the teachings and mysteries of Kabbalah.

Bakan (1965) stated plainly:

>…a full appreciation of the development of psychoanalysis is essentially incomplete unless it be viewed against the history of Judaism, and particularly against the history of Jewish mystical thought (p. ix).

Bakan, a psychoanalyst, concluded there was a "very profound: connection between psychoanalysis and Kabbalah.

Bakan stated:

>A Rebbe may share some qualities with a psychoanalyst. Both are experts about human nature as well as esoteric matters. For the Rebbe this includes spiritual or supra conscious realms, while for the psychoanalyst this includes inner reality, or the unconscious. And both encourage intense real and transference relationships among their adherents…I think that psychoanalysis is essentially a secular branch of Kabbalah, or to put it another way, psychoanalysis is secular Kabbalah (Ibid, p. 10, 38).

According to Bakan:

>...the contributions of Freud are to be understood largely as a contemporary version of, and a contemporary contribution to, the history of Jewish mysticism. Freud, consciously or unconsciously, secularized Jewish mysticism; and psychoanalysis can intelligently be viewed as such a secularization (Ibid, p. 25).

Berke (2015) argued:

>Freud's methods are astonishingly similar to those developed by the early Kabbalists, notably the thirteen-century Spanish Kabbalist, Rabbi Abraham Abulafia. Abulafia strove to "unseal the soul, to untie the knots which bind it...Basically he developed a theory of repression and a means to deal with the effects of repression six centuries before Freud (pp. 75-80).

Abulafia utilized a method of using associations as a way of meditation. Here, each "jump" or association opens a new sphere. Freud used this technique in free association.

The goal was to access hidden thoughts and feelings and bring them to understanding.

> The transformation from sick to sane took place when the concealed became revealed, when the unconscious became conscious, and his patients were able to "know" themselves (Berke, p. 410.

Freud's "attempt to reinterpret Judaism in a "scientific" manner" may be seen as "the creation of a secular, "scientific" Jewish theology (see K.)

> Finally, it is reasonable to conclude that Freud's real analysand was gentile culture, and that psychoanalysis was fundamentally an act of aggression toward that culture. The methodology and institutional structure of psychoanalysis may be viewed as attempts to brainwash gentile culture into passively accepting the radical criticism of gentile culture entailed by the fundamental postulates of psychoanalysis (Ibid. p. 134).

It may be seen that Freud's upbringing as well as his awareness of Jewish mysticism led him to formulations in many ways similar to those of the Gnostics. Perhaps most important of these is that there is a hidden (greater) reality behind the one we know—an essentially Greek idea.

Access to this realm is made by a process of profound inner exploration.

Related to such Greek ideas of the nature of reality, Nasios (see Nasios) wrote:

...the concept of "emanation" proposed by Kabbalah that God created the world in successive emanations is originally Greek. The philosopher Plotinus spoke about emanations in his work "Enneads". Kabbalah states that the human soul has three parts. Nefesh (lower self/animal nature), Ruach (middle soul, spirit, contains morals) and Neshamah (super-soul, holds intellect). This comes from Plato who said that the soul had three parts. Eros (cravings and desires), Themos (spiritedness, emotion) and Logos (reason and intellect, highest self).

Sepher Yetairah, author of the Book of Creation, an essential Kabbalistic text

...was influenced heavily by neoplatonsim, a late Greek philosophical school that combined elements of Plato with Oriental belief systems. Plato believed that our physical world is not the primary place of existence. He posited a "higher" world where the true forms exist. Our world is, he thought, only a mirror of the true world "above." Sefer Yetzirah placed these ideas into a Jewish framework. The work was back-dated and its authorship ascribed (in typical Kabbalistic fashion) to an authoritative Jewish figure, in this case Abraham (see History).

At any rate direct experience of the sacred was an important element in gnostic and mystical writings.

In this regard, Paul's own first-hand testimony cannot be emphasized enough, because it demonstrates that the first Christian Jews believed that they were recipients of ecstatic experiences both in the form of rapture events and invasions of heaven. In the context of this latter discourse, Paul also implies that he knows of other Christian Jews, perhaps associated with the mission of the Jerusalem church, who boast of mystical experiences. This is implied by the author of Colossians too. We have a quite strong tradition that the disciples and members of Jesus' family who formed the initial church in Jerusalem had visions of Jesus following his death. To Paul's first-hand witness we must also add the waking visions of John of Patmos and the dream visions of the Pastor Hermas. Of course, the evidence for mystical experience from second-hand accounts in the early Christian literature is staggering, ranging from the transfiguration of Jesus to the post-resurrection appearances to the vision of Stephen (see Definition).

The importance of experience in addition to knowledge is thus emphasized.

What these Jews and Christians seem to me to be saying is that intellectual pursuit of God and "truth" can only advance a person so far spiritually. It can get the person to the gate of the highest heavenly shrine, so to speak, but no further. They insist that knowledge of the sacred itself comes only through the direct experience of God, that is by actually meeting him face to face. It was this experiential encounter, they thought, that transformed them, that pulled them beyond the limits of their ordinary human senses and perceptions. This new godlike perspective, they believed, would lead to new understandings and revelations, allowing them to reinterpret the concealed truths and hidden histories locked within their sacred scriptures. So here lies the intersection between exegesis and experience (Ibid, see also Otto, 1958).

Philo of Alexandria was a Hellenized Jew provided a synthesis of Greek and Hebraic Ideas in the first century CE. It was Philo who developed much of the theological foundations of Christianity. In this way Greek ideas formed elemental conceptions of Christianity (see Philo).

To be sure Eliade (1957, 1963) did not think transcendent experiences were available to everyone. It required a certain facility.

We now know there is a difference between those with an open viewpoint and those with a closed viewpoint (Lakoff, 2016, Gill, 2016b). Here those with an open viewpoint welcome new input. These people are eager to embrace what is new and different. Closed people, on the other hand, prefer what is known, even traditional. They are more comfortable defending current knowledge against new ideas. Autocratic systems appeal to closed people. Egalitarian systems appeal to open people (Kaufman, 2013).

In this sense the gnostic texts appealed to more open people, whereas orthodox texts appealed to more closed people. Seen in this light these two approaches appeal to different sorts of world views.

In this sense, psychoanalysis too appeals to a certain kind of person. More concrete, scripted therapies appeal to another group, those poor at metaphorical usage. Further, if developmental studies are adequate, not all people are adept at abstract reasoning abilities. Attempts to restrict systems to either open or closed systems of necessity leaves out a significant portion of the population—as was the practice in the first two centuries CE.

The difficulties orthodox Christianity has had in our time may be due to its authoritarian character. While transcendence may interest people as well as finding expanded significance to their lives, the second century idea that this can only be accomplished by obedience to authority is highly questionable.

Further modern life requires a capacity to manage difference. Intersectionality demands an ability to reach beyond one's own area in order to adequately contact and understand another area. That is, one must move from what one knows to what one does not know. Openness is basic in this operation.

Openness is also an important capacity in the comprehension of metaphoric and figurative language.

> Truth did not come into the world naked, but
> it came in types and images. One will not
> receive truth in any other way (see Phillip).

This quote from the gnostic Gospel of Phillip suggests truth requires the ability to comprehend figurative language. Figurative language is precisely the device that allows for an expanded view (i.e., beyond one's familiar area).

An example is a poem by William Carlos Williams (see, Ellmann and O'Clair, pp. 288-289).

Tract

I will teach you my townspeople
how to perform a funeral
for you have it over a troop
of artists—
unless one should scour the world
you have the ground sense necessary.

See! the hearse leads.
I begin with a design for a hearse.
For Christ's sake not black—
nor white either—and not polished!
Let it be weathered—like a farm wagon—
with gilt wheels (this could be
applied fresh at small expense)
or no wheels at all:
a rough dray to drag over the ground.

Knock the glass out!
My God—glass, my townspeople!
For what purpose? Is it for the dead
to look out or for us to see
how well he is housed or to see
the flowers or the lack of them—
or what?
To keep the rain and snow from him?
He will have a heavier rain soon:

pebbles and dirt and what not.
Let there be no glass—
and no upholstery, phew!
and no little brass rollers
and small easy wheels on the bottom—
my townspeople, what are you thinking of?

A rough plain hearse then
with gilt wheels and no top at all.
On this the coffin lies
by its own weight.

              No wreaths please—
especially no hot house flowers.
Some common memento is better,
something he prized and is known by:
his old clothes—a few books perhaps—
God knows what! You realize
how we are about these things
my townspeople—
something will be found—anything
even flowers if he had come to that.
So much for the hearse.

For heaven's sake though see to the driver!
Take off the silk hat! In fact
that's no place at all for him—
up there unceremoniously
dragging our friend out to his own dignity!
Bring him down—bring him down!
Low and inconspicuous! I'd not have him ride
on the wagon at all—damn him—
the undertaker's understrapper!

Let him hold the reins
and walk at the side
and inconspicuously too!

Then briefly as to yourselves:
Walk behind—as they do in France,
seventh class, or if you ride
Hell take curtains! Go with some show
of inconvenience; sit openly—
to the weather as to grief.
Or do you think you can shut grief in?
What—from us? We who have perhaps
nothing to lose? Share with us
share with us—it will be money
in your pockets.
                              Go now
I think you are ready.

    This poem is typically regarded as an ars poetica, or advice on the art of writing a poem.   Here the funeral wagon is taken to be a metaphor for the poem. Williams is suggesting that it be plain, available to the elements and of simple design.   It should not be an artificially embellished display. The people should suffer a bit. The funeral wagon, the poem, should be simple and real, not dissevered from the struggles of life.

    The poem also may be read as advice about how to live an honest life.

    Are these interpretation factually true? This appears as an odd question. One would rather say the interpretations, as is the poem itself, are *evocative*. They open aspects of funerals, life, and poetry we may not have considered before.

American psychology in our time has struggled to be as scientific as possible. This in itself is somewhat ironic as psychology continues to confine itself to an essentially outmoded logical positivistic empirical position.

Such an approach has similarities to the orthodox efforts of the early Christians in its appeal to authority and tradition.

A more adequate view of language (Wittgenstein, 1953, Gadamer, 2008, Foucault, 1970, Derrida, 2016, et al) suggests extending scientific logic beyond (formal) positivist positions and allows for the inclusion of the proposition that what is seen depends upon where one stands.

Thus the positivist notion that the observer is independent from the observed is seen as not sustainable. Both the observer and the observed are related in an interactive dyad.

Following this logic it is not possible for all people to have the same interpretation of a poem, a gospel, or a psychoanalytic discovery. This is not so much a problem as it is the situation that obtains in the process of using language and language based processes in the contexts in which we find ourselves.

What we have taken as the *facts* of our lives and personalities are, in reality, *interpretations*. Discovering the problems in the interpretations upon which we have relied—and which have simultaneously led us astray, allows us to open newer interpretations of ourselves and our contexts.

This is the magic.

This is what the Greeks and mystics knew in the ancient world. There exists the possibility of a new life (an entirely new point of view). This new life was attained when the old life died (was surpassed). To the Greeks the resulting awareness was paradise. It was to trade the lower darkness for the higher light.

> Jesus said, "I shall give you what no eye has seen and what no ear has heard and what no hand has touched and what has never occurred to the human mind (Thomas, 17)."

Yet:

> He who knows the All but fails (to know) himself lacks everything (Thomas, 67).

REFRENCES

A. https://www.bc.edu/schools/stm/crossroads/resources/birthofjesus/intro/profile_the_gospelofmatthew.html

Abrams, M.H., Donaldson, E.T., Smith, H., Adams, R.M., Mond, S.H., Ford, G.H., and Daiches, D. (Eds.)   The Norton Anthology of English Literature. Vol. 2. Norton, 1962.

American Bible Society Good News for Modern Man: The New Testament in Today's English Version. 1966.

Bakan, D.   Sigmund Freud and the Jewish Mystical Tradition. Unknown, 1965.

Campbell, J. The Hero With a Thousand Faces. Princeton/ Bollengen, 1949/1972.

Campbell, J. The Inner Reaches of Outer Space: Metaphor as Myth and as Religion. Harper, 1986.

Campbell, J. The Hero's Journey. Harper. 1987.

Campbell, J.   Transformations of Myth Through Time. Harper, 1990.

Campbell, J. and Moyers, B.   The Power of Myth. Doubleday, 1988.

Camus, A. The Fall. Vintage. 1956.

Canney M. A. An Encyclooaedia of Religions. NAG, 1976.

Copleston, F. A History of Philosophy: Volume 1: Greece and Rome: Part One. Doubleday/Image, 1962.

Crossroads. http://www.bc.edu/schools/stm/crossroads/resources/birthofjesus/intro/the_dating_of_thegospels.html

Definition. http://www.marquette.edu/maqom/definition.pdf

Derrida, J. and Kaumf, P. A Derrida Reader: Between the Blinds. Columbia. 1991.

Derrida, J. and Spivak, G.C. Of Grammatology. Johns Hopkins, 2016.

Eliade, M. The Sacred and the Profane: The Nature of Religion. Harcourt, 1957/1987.

Eliade, M. Myth and Reality. Harper, 1963.

Foucault, M. The Order of Things: An Archeology of the Human Sciences. Vintage. 1970/1994.

Gabbard, G.O. Long-Term Psychodynamic Psychotherapy. American Psychiatric Press. 2004.

Gadamer, H-G.   Truth and Method (Bloomsbury Revelations). Bloomsbury Academic. 2013.

Gadamer, H-G. and Linge, D.E.   Philosophical Hermeneutics. California. 2008.

Gill, J.D.   The Eleusinian Mysteries.   In Mexico Papers, Volume Two, Create Space, 2016, pp. 11-38.

Gill, J.D.   Seeing in Intimacy and Psychotherapy.   Create Space, 2016b.

Ginsberg, H, and Opper S.   Piaget's Theory of Intellectual Development. Prentice-Hall, 1969.

Gospel of Phillip, in Robinson, J.M. (Ed.) The Nag Hammadi Library. Harper, 1977, p. 140.

Gospel of Thomas (T.O. Lambdin Translation).   http://www.marquette.edu/maqom/Gospel%20of%20Thomas%20Lambdin.pdf

Hatch. E.   The Influence of Greek Ideas on Christianity. Harper, 1957.

History. https://jewsforjesus.org/publications/issues/issues-v12-n02/a-history-of-the-kabbalah/

Jung, C.G., and Kerenyi, C.   Essays on a Science of Mythology: The Myth of the Divine Child and the Mysteries of Elsusis. Princeton/Bollingen, 1949/1978.

J1. http://www.abc.net.au/religion/stories/s796551.htm

J2. http://www.historyworld.net/wrldhis/ PlainTextHistories.asp?historyid=aa42#ixzz52IBewBFU

K. http://www.kevinmacdonald.net/chap4.pdf

Kabbalah. https://kabbalah.com/en/master-kabbalists/the-zohar

Kaufman, S. B. Openness to New Experience and Creative Achievement. Scientific American, 11-25-2013.

Kerenyi, C. Eleusis: Archetypal Image of Mother and Daughter. Princeton/Bolligen. 1967.

Kraft, J. Judaism and Psychology. https://www.myjewishlearning.com/article/judaism-and-psychology/

Kuperman, L. The Jewish Psychologists from Freud to Dr. Ruth. http://www.larrykuperman.com/wp-content/uploads/2015/08/The-Jewish-Psychologists1.pdf

Lakoff, G. Understanding Trump. Political Comments, 07-23-16. https://georgelakoff.com/2016/07/23/ understanding-trump-2/

Langman, P. "White Culture, Jewish Culture and the Origins of Psychotherapy. In Psychotherapy, 1997, pp.207-218.

Nasios, A. http://thatstotallytarot.com/kabbalah-neo-platonism/

News. Good News for Modern Man: The New Testament in Today's English Version. American Bible Society, 1966.

Ogden, T. H. The Primitive Edge of Experience. Aronson. 1989.

Otto, R. The Idea of the Holy: an Inquiry into the Non-rational factor in the Idea of the Divine and its Relation to the Rational. Oxford, 1923/1958.

Pagels, E. The Gnostic Gospels. Vintage, 1979.

Pagels, E.   The Johnnine   Gospel in Gnostic Exegesis. Scholars Press, 1989.

Pagels, E.   Beyond Belief: The Secret Gospel of Thomas. Random House, 2003.

Philip. The Gospel of Philip. http://gnosis.org/naghamm/gop.html

Philo. https://www.iep.utm.edu/philo/

Philologos. https://forward.com/culture/177588/how-greek-philosophy-influenced-both-christian-and/

Plato, The Republic, Book VII, in Great Dialogues of Plato, (tr.) W.H.D. Rouse. Mentor. 1956.

Robinson, J. M. (Ed.) The Nag Hammadi Library. Harper. 1977.

Roith, E. The Riddle of Freud: Jewish Influences on his Theory of Female Sexuality. Tavistock, 1987.

Scott, W. Hermetica: The Ancient Greek and Latin Writings which Contain Religious or Philosophic Teachings Ascribed to Hermes Trismegistus. Shambala. 1993.

Slavet, E. Freud's Theory of Jewishness: For Better or Worse. https://divinity.uchicago.edu/sites/default/files/imce/pdfs/webforum/112011/Slavet%20Final.pdf

T. www.goodnewsinc.net/othbooks/thomas.html

Thilly, F. and Wood, L. A History of Philosophy. Holt. 1957.

Thomas. The Gospel of Thomas (Lambdin Translation). http://www.gnosis.org/naghamm/gthlamb.html

Williams, W. C. Tract. in Ellmann, R., and O'Clair, R. (Eds.) The Norton Anthology of Modern Poetry. Norton, 1973, pp. 288-289.

Wittgenstein, L. Philosophical Investigations. Macmillan. 1953.

Wittgenstein, L. The Blue and Brown Books. Harper, 1958/1965.

Zohar. http://www.jewishvirtuallibrary.org/the-zohar

GNOSTIC ADDENDUM

Faith receives, love gives. No one will be able to receive without faith. No one will be able to give without love. Because of this, in order that we may indeed receive, we believe, and in order that we may love, we give, since if one gives without love, he has no profit from what he has given.

The Gospel of Philip

Studying ancient texts made it clear to me how unaware the culture of my youth truly was. Surrounded by people who were utterly convinced in a rigid sort of orthodox, if not fundamentalistic, notion of religion, there was no home at the inn.

They all seemed so *convinced*. And the message was that one should submit to their views. They were angry about this. Not to submit was to be cast forever into "outer darkness." Yet what were those views? God is strict. God has a plan for you, which you must follow precisely, as any deviation will meet with God's wrath. God will especially be wrathful to those who drink alcohol, smoke tobacco, or who are not monogamous.

Church services were scarcely sacred. People with poor cultural or classical education as a rule opined on topics as they saw fit. We were to follow dutifully in order to receive our reward. Further, the devil was all around. One had to be forever vigilant to escape his grasp—as those who were speaking felt they surely had. If we followed God's plan, we would be included; if we followed our own plan, we were doomed.

At no point did the discussion lift to a higher order. If an attempt at this was made, it was largely a keromic, psychic sort of attempt*. Eternal life was something that was hooked onto the end of this one. When someone died, we were to be joyful, as he or she was clearly in a better place. Physically. God was male. His son was male. Sanctified people in the church were male. Women were to follow (Paul's Epistle to the Ephesians read literally). Children were to honor (obey) their father and mother—and give them no lip.

The eucharist was supposed to be the body and blood of Christ, but no one knew just how this was to be. It was simply done. Judgement was everywhere. Narcissism was its structure. These were the chosen people.

I don't know how many of these people knew much about Greek religion or metaphysics. They were people akin to unenlightened masses. The world was their place. Neither gnosis, logos, nor anthropos formed any part of their views. "Get in the boat and stay in the boat."

Religion, as it was related to us, was ominous, autocratic, and full of fear. The threat of punishment was everywhere. Those who went astray were to be punished for "all of eternity." That was a real place, beyond this one, very bad.

Sweetness was largely reserved for children. The baby Jesus was their friend. God wanted to dance with them in golden meadows—unless they were bad. Didn't they want that?

This was a religion that was entirely profane though it mouthed a certain material sort of spirituality. The sacred, essentially, had no place. Further, other religions were held to be inferior and inadequate.

I am left to wonder how many of these people actually read the New Testament. If they did, what did they read? What did they glean from it? That they were right?

How did they interpret the beginning lines in the Gospel of John?

In the beginning was the logos, and the logos was with God and the logos was God. He was with God in the beginning. Through him all things were made; without him nothing was made. In him was life, and that life was the light of all mankind. The light shines in the darkness, and the darkness has not overcome it (John 1:1-5).

What did they think?

They likely did not think of the logos as an emanation of the pleromic aion (see Pagels, 1989). Nor did they imagine that God, who is beyond comprehension or extension, produced the logos to function as the creator. And since the logos emerged from God, the logos and God had elements in common. The understanding logos was the light that made comprehension possible.

What characterized these church people the most was how rigid they were. There were no doubts admitted in their beliefs, and those beliefs demanded compliance. Nonetheless, the compliance they demanded was to an amorphously defined position. The compliance was more important than the position.

The deity these people imagined was a projection of themselves. Their deity was also autocratic, judgmental, and punitive. At the same time, this deity was somehow loving but only to those who were obedient.

Something always seemed wrong with this position, but none of us knew quite what it was. Why all this autocracy? Were we really that stupid? That bad? We were reassured our questions were a weakness.

Furthermore, such views and attitudes were all around us. Virtually everyone we knew believed and followed them. It was not socially wise to show disagreement or, often, even curiosity.

For many, if not most, of us the first time we had any notion of a different view was in college. There was when we began to read widely. We studied thinking and philosophy. The difference between what the gnostics called a psychic and pneumatic sensibility began to emerge. Eliade's (1957) distinction between the sacred and the profane could be seen in a larger context. To be sure, facility with the linguistic device of metaphor varied between us. The metaphysics of Plato made sense or it did not—aside from its truth value. Poetry resonated or did not. Higher math was exciting, or it was not. Psychoanalysis worked for us, or it did not.

Pagels (1981, 1988, 1989, 1992, 2005) drove the point home for me and made the lack we had suffered clear.

The rejection and condemnation of gnostic texts by the orthodox Christians during the first period of Christianity had, I could attest, been remarkably successful. The Christian church had flourished in its psychic interpretation, the gnostic interpretations having been banned and/or destroyed.

The discovery at Nag Hammadi changed all this. Here were the very texts that had been condemned and/or destroyed by the Christians in the course of the development of orthodoxy. The recovered gnostic texts spoke, as it were, a whole different language. And they spoke about a whole different religious view—one that actually made sense.

The goal was gnosis (awareness, enlightenment) instead of obedience. Attaining this required moving beyond the psychic (material) interpretations in order to come to the pneumatic (gnostic) interpretations. God is beyond knowing. (The worshiped God is the Demiurge.) The pleroma was a spiritual dimension of enlightenment. The route was largely inner as opposed to being largely outer.

Condemned in the early Christian period as religion for intellectuals, gnostic views were primarily Greek as opposed to Hebraic. Distinctions from the mystery religions were involved. The Greek notion of the differences between the physical world and the transcendent world were pivotal.

The gnostic idea, according to Valentinius (see V, Thomassen, 2008), is that there are three basic levels of awareness.

The first of these is hylic. This is akin to hard materialism. It is a capacity shorn of all spiritual ability—an empirical-only realm. Persons in the hylic area did not choose to be there. They are there based on their natural capacity.

The second level is psychic, the kenoma. Here people are able to comprehend spiritual things but only through the following of dictates of the law and prophesies. Group worship is the essential religious act. These people must choose to orient themselves either to a higher plane or be identified with a lower plane. In other words, they are keen either to read about the foreign land or not, but they are not yet able to travel there.

The third level is pneumatic, the pleroma, where awareness has been derived from the connotation of the metaphor. Such persons did not achieve this position as a result of obedience or effort. The ability is part of his or her nature. It is discovered. The capacity to comprehend and experience pneumatic elements is what defines this group.

In light of such distinctions Orthodox Christianity may be thought of as largely composed of psychic members. These persons range from higher-order mystic Christians to lower-order fundamentalists. Belonging to the organization and adhering to its commandments (worship) are highly valued. This is a kind of loyalty to the rituals of the organization that brings rewards.

Gnostics, on the other hand, have attained a personal awareness that is akin to metaphysical insight. The elements of the physical and spiritual regions are open to them. Having such gnosis allows them to grasp their immersion in spiritual or higher-order being. In a real sense, they have left their bodies for this awareness.

The gnostic ideas were in many ways akin to those of the Eleusinian mysteries see Kereynyi, 1967, Gill, 2016). At the height of those mystery rites the Hierophant (high priest) raised an ear of corn. The act was accompanied by a huge fire and a thunderous gong. This was the message. On the lower level the kernels of corn, now harvested and therefore dead, are planted in the soil. From them grow new life. On the higher level what is material (the corn/the initiates), having gained entrance to the higher regions, sprout awareness of eternal dimensions.

In both instances life comes from death. That is the miracle. The old has to die so the new can begin. This is an essential message throughout the Pauline letters.

What I did not realize was that a similar process was happening in me. The old religion had to die so the greater awareness could begin. It is a bit like Zen satori where individual distinction melts into universal awareness.

It seemed so simple when explained.

But it was never explained. No one around me in my childhood was conversant with any of these ideas—or, if they were, I didn't know it. They would likely have thought they were stupid—as they differed from what they knew. They would have argued against them—almost reflexively. These were the people who were my superiors and were convinced they knew more and that they were right. And I would have a difficult time explaining such views to (most of) them. Even if they were somehow interested.

A large part of why this would be true is that these people were not given to metaphor and symbolic reading as a rule. Nor were they open to new information. Concrete in their speech and reading, they tended to also be concrete in their religion. Hermeneutics were not their bag. Obedience to the law was closer.

> Although they knew God, they did not glorify him as God, or thank him, but became vain in their imagination, and their foolish heart was darkened. Claiming to be wise, they became fools, and exchanged the glory of the incorruptible God for the image of the anthropos...and exchanged the truth of God for a lie, and they revered and worshiped the creation and not the one who created, who is blessed among the aions (Romans, 1:21-25).**

The religion surrounding my childhood experience was fiercely based on obedient rituals, beliefs, and worship. Members were following the plan that had been dictated (revealed) to them.

Psychic Christians worship the Demiurge as God instead of "Christ the Logos." This is to fail to understand the metaphor of the Demiurge as God.

The law was designed for those in the kenoma, not those of the pleroma. Psychic worshipers, being unable to grasp issues symbolically, must have a way to find worthiness.

For the one who works, the reward is not accounted according to grace but according to obligation. And to the one who does not work, but believes on him who justifies the unholy, his faith is accounted for righteousness. So also David speaks of the blessedness of the one whom God accounts righteous apart from works: "blessed are those whose transgressions are forgiven, whose sins are covered; blessed is the one to whom the Lord does not impute sin (Romans 4:4-8).

Thus there are two paths described here. On the lower plane, one is to follow the law and do good works. On the higher plane, one participates directly in the higher order.

In other words;

...if we have died with Christ, we know that we also shall live with him...the death he died he died to sin...

...but the life he lives he lives to God. So also you must consider yourselves dead to sin, but alive to God (Romans 6:3-11)

The "death" about which Paul speaks here is to the concrete realm. The "life" is the life of the symbolic referent.

According to Paul all commandments are summed up in the words "you shall love your neighbor as yourselves... love is the fulfillment (pleroma) of the law (Romans 13:8-10)."

This does not mean love your neighbor who agrees with you. It does not mean love your neighbor who lives in your area. It does not mean love your neighbor who is of the same race, same sex, same SES, or who smells good. It means love *all* persons.

And yet:

> Let the one who eats not despise the one who abstains, and the one who abstains not judge the one who eats, for God has welcomed him. Who are you to judge one who belongs to another? One stands or falls before his own Lord (Romans 14:1).

Thus those who are strong are to help those who are weak and not seek to please themselves.

> We do speak sophia among the initiates, but not the wisdom of this age or the archons of this age, who are passing away. But we

speak the hidden sophia of God in a mystery, which God ordained before the aions for our glory. None of the archons of this age knew this: had they known it, they would not have crucified the Lord of glory (1 Corinthians, 2:6-8).

The archons, unaware of the mystery of the Mother Sophia, are kept from awareness of their limitations. That is, what is beyond them is incomprehensible to them *even though* available.

For the psychic does not receive the things of the spirit of God: they are foolishness to him, and he cannot know them, because they are pneumatically discerned. The pneumatic on the other hand discerns all things, but himself is discerned by no one. For "who has known the mind of the Lord, and who may instruct him?" But we have the mind of Christ (1 Corinthians, 2: 14-16)!

The difference is somewhat akin to one who has travelled in a distant land versus one who has read about it. What one knows at a personal level is different from what another may only imagine.

Love bears all things, believes all things, hopes all things, suffers all things. Love never fails. If there are prophecies, they shall cease; if there are tongues, they shall cease; if there is gnosis, it will disappear. For now we know in part and we prophecy in part. But when the perfect comes, what is partial shall disappear (1 Corinthians, 13:7-10).

When the psychics are granted the perception of the pneumatics, all will be clear.

The pneumatic situation is made clearer in a passage from Galatians:

For through the law I died to the law, that I might live to God. I have been crucified with Christ; I live, yet it is no longer I, but Christ who lives in me. What I now live in the flesh, I live in faith in the son of God, who has loved me, and has given himself for me. I do not reject the grace of God; for if righteousness is through the law, Christ died in vain (Galatians, 2: 19-21).

In other words Paul here claims that what was hylic in him has been consumed, and what was psychic has been clarified. He now lives in pneumatic awareness (Christ lives in him).

...the fruit of the spirit is love, joy, peace, patience, kindness, goodness, faithfulness, gentleness, self-control: against such there is no law. Those who belong to Christ Jesus have crucified the flesh with its passions and desires (Galatians, 5: 24).

The point is that the psychics worship physical elements, which are only images of what exists in the pleroma (see also Hebrews, 8: 1-5). The demiurge, whom the psychics worship as God, is not the true creator (see also John, 1: 1-5).

What a clever trap I had found! The people in my background were not significantly educated in religion or philosophy. They simply listened to each other. Their awareness encompassed the entirety of their knowledge. They knew no more than this. I cannot blame them for what they did not know.

It is the defensiveness of their not knowing—seen by them as certainty of what they did know—that was the problem. They needed to think they had the truth with a capitol T. In this they mimicked the early Christians who developed the orthodoxy. They had to be the authorities. Perhaps being the authorities meant more to them than being open to discovering new things. They had a religion complete to themselves, they imagined, that needed nothing else.

It is the case that religion has largely been set aside in many modern intellectual arenas. This is likely due in a large part to such oafish demands of rigid psychics. What works for the psychic power structure routinely does not work for highly intelligent, intuitive, and creative persons who are adept at metaphorical and symbolic thinking. Such people excel by discovering and creating elements beyond in-the-box thinking. As Gilbert Ryle said somewhere, "There is one person to whom it is impertinence to suggest he stay on the curb, and that is the pathfinder."

In life as in psychotherapy, we advance when we are able to transcend the places where we have been caught. Once such transcendence has been achieved, it is difficult to relate, without remainder, to those who remain in regions we have left behind. We have moved to a newer level, and we have visited a new land.

REFERENCES

Campbell, J. The Inner Reaches of Outer Space: Metaphor as Myth and as Religion. Harper, 1986.

Eliade, M. The Sacred and the Profane: The Nature of Religion. Harcourt, 1957/1987.

Kerenyi, C. Eleusis: Archetypal Image of Mother and Daughter. Princeton/Bollengen, 1967.

Gill, J.D. Mexico Papers. Vol. 2. Create Space, 2016.

Jung, C.G., and Kerenyi, C. Essays on a Science of Mythology: The Myth of the Divine Child and the Mysteries of Elsusis. Princeton/Bollingen, 1949/1978.

Pagels, E. The Gnostic Gospels. Vintage, 1981.

Pagels, E. Adam, Eve, and the Serpent. Vintage, 1988.

Pagels, E. The Johannine Gospel in Gnostic Exegesis. Scholars Press, 1989.

Pagels, E. The Gnostic Paul: Gnostic Exegesis of the Pauline Letters. Continuum, 1992.

Pagels, E. Beyond Belief: The Secret Gospel of Thomas. Random House, 2005.

Thilly, F. and Wood, L.   A History of Philosophy.   Holt. 1957.

Thomassen, E.   The Spiritual Seed: The Church of the "Valentinians." Brill Academic Publications, 2008.

V   http://www.gnostic-jesus.com/gnostic-jesus/Syrian-Egyptian/ Valentinian-view.html

* See The Gnostic Gospels and Psychoanalytic Awareness in this volume.

** Translations appear in Pagels 1989, 1992.

LITTLE NOTE ON POETRY

I'm looking for the kind of silence
that yields clarity.

—Tracy K. Smith

Poetry is the hardest thing. It is a vast and rich place that is explored and seen differently by everyone who comes to it. And it is only reasonable this should be so. Each of us is an amalgam of different experiences, histories, longings, and tastes. We find the poems that resonate with who we are.

The study of poetry can be different. Here the toad from a real garden is laid out on the table for dissection. We separate its parts and learn their names and functions—their contribution to the whole. We are able to identify these on an exam. If we persist in this project, we become more knowledgeable about toads. We develop finer and finer distinctions. We have a sense of where each example fits in the *genus*.

We may attempt to write poetry. We attempt to say something in a poem that has its own integrity. We are conscious of how it sounds. We try different arrangements. We search for something fresh. We may seek a certain style. We hand our poems around. We want to hear what people think.

And we read poetry. It intrigues and delights us. We read and read and read. Somewhere we realize we have developed certain tastes, preferences, and habits.

In both the poetry that I read and study as well as the poetry I write there is an attempt to make that which is beyond the ordinary manifest. This is a kind of writing that is its own thing. And, I have come to see, it demands its own capacity.

Readers, after all, have their own capacities. Some are highly educated in poetry, some are almost illiterate. Some like strong poems, some like those more refined. Long, short, ironic, glum, trivial, or profound, the focus can be anything.

Readers have different abilities, different capacities in what they can see. Metaphor, for example, comes easily and quickly to some but is almost gibberish to others.

Similarly, understanding may be insightful and profound or practically banal.

One way to describe these differences comes from philosophical and theological notions of Valentinus (see V, Pagels, 1989, 1992). Here the group of followers was divided into three subgroups relative to their perceptive abilities.

The first, and lowest order group, were the *hylics*. These were those whose perceptual universe primarily consisted of things of this world. These were the empiricists. The facts and events of the world were the extent of their occupation. "Higher" or spiritual elements were not routinely part of their lives.

The next group was the *kenoma*. This group was like the first except they were aware of spiritual matters and longed to experience them. Such experience, however, was largely denied them in its direct form, and so they were left with rituals of worship and observances as their spiritual life.

The third group was the *pleroma*. These were people who were able to directly experience spiritual things and participate immediately in them. Such ability was not learned, nor was it the result of programs of worship.

Obviously, these differences were significantly related to linguistic capacity. Fluency with the grammar of metaphor played an essential role as did increasing abilities in abstract thought.

Metaphor is the essential tool of the emotions. While the denotation of the metaphor may be a physical fact, the connotation is always something evoked. Extended, an entire realm may be evoked.

Capacity to extend into the abstract realm may allow discovery of breadth as well as depth. The language of rapture and grief illustrates this range.

Elements from one level may be uninteresting or not even understandable to someone from another level. Such elements, which may be wrenchingly profound to some, may be simply silly or gibberish to others.

Still, the poetry audience contains all these different abilities. Poems written for one group will be difficult for another. They will seem alien, off somehow.

Following the above logic, the *special place* may be considered as an experience suspended within daily events. Akin to a secret garden, it is especially to be found in afternoons. The special place is definitely interior, an amalgam of thoughts and feelings at some kind of reverie. The special place is separate from other people and their comings and goings. It is at once more refined and yet more simple than average events.

In the language of Valentinus, the special place is related to the pleroma.

The special place opens in childhood during those long times when others have no time for one. It opens in imagination. What can't be found in the surround or in interactions is available in the imagination. If this is allowed to grow, it can become an entire kingdom, vaguely defined, but rich and rewarding.

Love is to be found in the special place. The sacred is to be found. It is what is called deeper meaning, and the possession of it earns one the label: sensitive. Soon the special place becomes the deepest thing, that location where significance is most profound. One begins to notice the times when it is most resonant: nature, empty chapels, the tenderness of children.

Different from displays that are loud or flashy, the special place finds home in emptiness. The hours in-between. It often takes on colors of a sunset or a waiting vista. Not everyone is drawn to the special place. Usually it is those who have spent a long time watching. Young people who spend time in libraries or some solitary pursuit that allows pause.

There are poems that rise in the special place. These are poems that seek to resonate with others from the special place. That is their main audience. Perhaps someone not routinely from the special place will be struck, and a recognition will occur. The importance of the special place will be understood and its significance honored.

An example is 'Ubung Am Klavier' (Piano Practice) by Rilke:

Der Sommer summt. Der Nachmittag macht müde;
sie atmete verwirrt ihr frisches Kleid

und legte in die triftige Etude
die Ungeduld nach einer Wirklichkeit,

die kommen konnte morgen, heute Abend,
die vielleicht da war, die man nur verbarg;
und vor den Fenstern, hoch and alles habend,
empfand sie plötzlich den verwohnten Park.

Da brach sie ab; schaute hinaus, verschränkte
die Hände, wünschte sich ein langes Buch
und schob auf einmal den Jasmingeruch
erzürnt zurück. Sie fand, dass er die krankte.

This poem may be translated as follows:

Summer hums. Afternoon grows tired;
Confused she fluffs her fresh dress
and into the stiff etude she sets
an impatience for something real

that could come tomorrow, this evening,
is perhaps there now yet only hidden
and suddenly through the window, high
and rich, she senses the indulged park.

She breaks off playing, looks outside,
folds her hands, wishes for a long book
and then pushes back the jasmine scent
She finds the fragrance hurts.

It could be argued this poem captures a small moment that in turn reflects an entire state of living. Decadent in its elegance, it speaks of a faint sadness that is at once recognizable and rare. It is almost too fragile to read, let alone speak.

The poem speaks to those who have known such moments, as, indeed, a good many people have. It is that time between when it seems one is always waiting.

Another example is by Philip Larkin:

GOING

There is an evening coming in
Across the fields, one never seen before,
That lights no lamps.

Silken it seems at a distance, yet
When it is drawn up over the knees and breast
It brings no comfort.

Where has the tree gone, that locked
Earth to the sky? What is under my hands,
That I cannot feel?

What loads my hands down?

Here emptiness is represented in its mystery, its opening, the reason to experience it so completely.

Not all poems, certainly, rise from the special place. Many deliberately do not. There are thing-in-themselves poems, outrageous poems, real toads in real gardens poems, clever word-craft poems, long sweeping epic poems, occasional poems, and abstract reference poems—among many.

All of these have their place, as do poems from the special place.

In school we were taught to develop a fear of mushiness and sentimentality. And for good reason. The special place need not contain these elements. There are many non-mushy and non-sentimental ways to write about, say, tenderness, the experience of being human, solitude, rapture, &c.

As a culture we have tended to admire what is narcissistic and superior. Certainly, academia is a place where such traits thrive. In those places where strength is admired, there is sometimes no place for what might be called, simply, honest. It is routinely important for narcissistic defenses to eschew such things, and we have a long history of excluding voices.

Recent developments in feminism, post-modernism, and intersectionality have emphasized voices that have routinely been left out in our cultural accounts. As these voices are heard, the culture widens.

Poems from the special place tend to be private. They are an evocation of a space and mood that lies behind objective scenes. An example is from James Schuyler (1993):

SUNDAY

The mint bed is in
bloom: lavender haze
day. The grass is
more than green and
throws up sharp and
cutting lights to
slice through the
plane tree leaves. And
on the cloudless blue
I scribble your name.

Schuyler is famous for his embodiment of sophistication in what appears commonplace. Like other New York poets he evokes a world of being outside.

The poems of Hart Crane (1958) also routinely evoke worlds beyond their referents. Yet in Crane's case, the language is ornate and classical as in this example of the mystery in erotic aftermath:

and where death, if shed,
Presumes no carnage, but this single change, —

Upon the steep floor flung from dawn to dawn
The silken skilled transmemberment of song.

Such poems, whatever else they may accomplish, offer momentary epiphanies in the hugeness of time. They display, if you will, a transcendent, quiet power. It is as if a voice, behind or beyond daily concerns speaks its truth— the little part of us that matters, that has always mattered.

And for this reason, the voice opens a sensibility that thrives in stillness, in empty places, and in that space when everything else pauses. It is not a voice of authority or erudition. It is, rather, a voice that challenges these.

In a large sense such poems are a message from beyond routine events. They are often even beyond routine literary dimensions, as they attempt to open what lies behind and beyond them as well.

Peter Everwine (1977) wrote:

NIGHT

In the lamplight falling
on the white tablecloth
my plate,
my shining loaf of quietness.

I sit down.
Through the open door

all the absent I love enter
and we eat.

Eliade (1957) made a distinction between the sacred and the profane.   The profane is physical, empirical, and external.   The sacred is spiritual and transcendent.   The spiritual lies behind or beyond the physical.   Seen in this light the special place is a spiritual dimension, though not necessarily in a religious sense.   (Actually, orthodox religions tend to be profane in this distinction, though they envision spiritual matters.)

Both art and the sacred metaphorically tap into a dimension that lies beyond description.   They are modalities that evoke a connotation beyond their denotation. As such, they attempt to tap into an experience of living.   Metaphor allows a reach beyond history.   It speaks to how it felt beyond an account of what happened. This in turn preserves and illuminates what is distinctly human.

Culture is made up of both empirically focused as well as emotionally focused dimensions.   It contains people who routinely prefer and are largely adept at one dimension or another.   By use of metaphor the dimensions are linked. The empirical dimension is the denotation and the emotional dimension is the connotation of the metaphor. This is how art compels us: by inducing us to experience the dimension of significance that lies behind or beyond what otherwise occupies our attention.

At its most profound, what lies behind informs and deepens what is seen. It is not the only element that matters, but it opens a dimension nothing else can. It is, we could say, another voice in the overall harmony.

REFERENCES

Crane, H.   The Complete Poems of Hart Crane. Doubleday, 1958.

Edelman, L. Transmemberment of Song: Hart Crane's Anatomies of Rhetoric and Desire. Stanford, 1987.

Eliade, M.   The Sacred and the Profane: The Nature of Religion. Harcourt, 1957/1987.

Everwine, P. Keeping the Night. Atheneum, 1977.

Rilke, R.M. Gesammelte Gedichte. Insel-Verlag, 1962.

Schuyler, J. Collected Poems. FSG, 1993.

SILENCE AT THE CENTER OF TIME

The experience of the self in its own space opens to the world. This is when it has itself entirely to itself as a living fact. The knowledge the self has is lined on its own shelves, and the emotions of the self are gathered around.

This is the self, as it were, pulled back from activity, from engagement in sectors of life. Here, the self feels itself *in potentia* and also at one with itself. The self is able to settle in its own space. Like a person alone in a house, the self is aware of all it has been able to discover.

The attitude of the self in this silence is open. Nothing it can know is excluded. It feels its life intensely, and it rolls its objects in its hands.

The self, at such moments, has no past and no future. The seasons of itself are open and on view. It is out of this dimension that the silence opens. The self is at once its creator and its recipient. Memories, thoughts, and wishes arise in this space, but the self is primarily focused on its living and its ontology.

Cast in this light the self is an event in time. It is also the standpoint of its own experience of time. In this way time opens and travels outward from the self's experience. Time is the dimension of its extension, the scope of its opportunity at being. Such a gift of life is not lost on the self nor is the sobering comparison it makes with others.

The self is not alone in its aloneness.

When life bears down too strongly, it is the space at the center of the self where there is refuge. In this place the self can begin to regenerate itself and focus its efforts anew. Sometimes this takes a long time as the self tries to find a path that will allow it to function while, at the same time, maintaining its own integrity.

When wounded the self gathers into itself and waits. When broken it pauses to heal. When there is no tomorrow the self becomes its own tomorrow. When there is no life possible the self opens.

The self has its own spaces that are felt in triumph or in rapture. It sees such things as moments in its span of time, and it softens them.

The self is most at home with nothing but itself and its time. Aware of the danger of excessive self-focus, the self nevertheless comprises the area of its own reference. Year by year it finds itself again. Like a constant shadow even in the brightest hours, the self expresses its own dimension.

The self exists in its silence at the center of time as that is its experience of its position. From it, time opens out in every direction. From its center life opens out. It is in this sense all time and all extension will perish with the self. Its *take* will vanish. Nor will this space be available to others, except through the vehicle of what the self has been able to accomplish. In this, the self will be seen to have tried to join with time itself.

There is, in a sense, a communality of selves. It constitutes what Wittgenstein called a form of life. It is the way we are. Where it seems missing, we count it as a loss. Wilfred Owen (1961) wrote:

> ...cursed are dullards whom no cannon stuns,
> That they should be as stones.
> Wretched are they, and mean
> With paucity that never was simplicity.
> By choice they made themselves immune
> To pity and whatever moans in man
> Before the last sea and the hapless stars;
> Whatever mourns when many leave these shores;
> Whatever shares
> The eternal reciprocity of tears.

The self has learned to eschew efforts to corrupt it from itself. It has found ways to gracefully excuse itself from glittery games, loud voices, and clamor. The self has found a way to be connected and also disconnected. Plugged in so as not to be widely considered odd, the self has its little escapes, its silent afternoons, its late night walks.

Finding the silence of another self is a transcendent moment. There, in that juncture, silences can meet. And then the silences can grow. This is the case in the deepest love, in quiet interactions with a child.

Still the self maintains its own dimension, its own property. There it retreats to ground itself and re-found its own integrity. When another's silence means as much as the self's own silence, a fundamental connection has taken place. This will last as long as the selves involved remain true to themselves.

It is not wise to deny the self its own time, its own time with itself in the silence. That is where the greenest leaves are able to open and grow. Still, the self, once able to achieve the center of this silence, must not remain there. It is only in interaction with context that the self learns how to calibrate itself.

For if the self is not of use to someone else, it cannot be of use to itself. If the self is only of use to someone else, it loses itself.

What is important about us is what we know we do not know.

The time one has is for discovery and awareness of the self, its passages, and its dimensions. Where the center of the self rises, there life rises and may be known it its purest form. When the self is aware it is always morning. When shadows cross the self, it is always afternoon.

The experience of pain changes the self and deepens it. The life of pain and the life of not-pain is not the same life. It is pain that teaches us the importance of things. It courses throughout the self and colors it. Those who have been left out because of pain have a wisdom there is no other way to attain. These selves carry an acute view of experience.

In the space of its own time, the self becomes the experience of life. It is but a taste, but the self has a desire to grasp it and make it manifest. From the alchemy of the self's interaction with time what is eternal is created. This, simple in itself, affects what matters. It is almost too much to grasp.

All selves are able to resonate at this level if they have been able to pause enough to find themselves. It is in that silence that life opens its true moment.

REFERENCES

Blunden, E. (Ed.)   The Poems of Wilfred Owen.   Chatto and Windus, 1961.

ABOUT THE AUTHOR

J.D. Gill is a clinical psychologist at the University of Utah. She is an Adjunct Associate Professor of Psychology, a Clinical Professor of Counseling Psychology, and an Adjunct Associate Professor of Psychiatry in the University of Utah School of Medicine. Dr. Gill maintains a busy clinical practice.

Dr. Gill has degrees in English Literature, Philosophy, Psychology, and two post docs in psychoanalytic psychotherapy. She studied in the Writing Program at the University of Utah. She has been a practicing psychologist for over forty years and has presented over five hundred seminars, lectures, workshops, and papers. A world traveler, Dr. Gill has actively sought to experience multiple viewpoints and perspectives.

www.ingramcontent.com/pod-product-compliance
Lightning Source LLC
Chambersburg PA
CBHW062201280526
45788CB00001B/391